INDUSTRIAL ENGINEERING AND MANAGEMENT

P. SIVASANKARAN, B.E., M.E., Ph. D
Associate Professor
Department of Mechanical Engineering
Christ College of Engineering and Technology
Pondicherry

AMAZON

USA, UK, Denmark, Spain, France, Italy,
Netherland, Japan, Brazil, Canada, Mexico,
India and Australia

Industrial Engineering and Management

P.Sivasankaran

ISBN: 978-93-5737-018-9

The export rights of this book are vested solely with the Amazon

Published by Amazon Self-Publishing

Sales Websites: amazon.com, amazon.co.uk, amazon.de, amazon.es, amazon.fr, amazon.it, amazon.nl, amazon.co.jp, amazon.com.br, amazon.ca, amazon.com.mx, amazon.in, amazon.com.au

Published by Dr.P. Sivasankaran, First Floor, No.20, Second Cross Street, Kalaivani Nagar, Pethichettipet, Lawspet, Pondicherry – 605 008.

Dedicated to all my teachers, in Specific the following professors.

Dr.P.Shahabudeen, Professor (Retd.)
Industrial Engineering Department
Anna University
Chennai

Dr.T. Sornakumar, Professor (Retd.)
Mechanical Engineering Department
Thiagarajar College of Engineering
Madurai

CONTENTS

CONTENTS

CONTENTS

CONTENTS

CONTENTS

PREFACE

Population growth, modern living, and the increasing demand for basic necessities compel businesses to be more efficient and effective in their manufacturing and service operations if they are to produce goods and provide services at prices that will satisfy a wide range of customers amid intense competition. Industrial engineering and management cover the essential concepts and methods for running businesses successfully. Dr.P. Sivasankaran, who had taught this subject of industrial engineering and management for more than a decade at Anna University and its affiliated colleges as well as affiliated colleges of Pondicherry University, had recognized the need for a comprehensive text combining these two disciplines and had written this as a result of his rich teaching and research experience. This will serve as a text book for the students of B.E./B.Tech./B.S. (Mechanical Engineering, Production Engineering, Industrial Engineering, Mechatronics Engineering and Industrial Systems Engineering), M.E./M.Tech./M.S. (Industrial Engineering, Manufacturing Systems Management, Production/ Manufacturing Engineering, and Industrial Systems Engineering) and M.B.A.

This text begins with plant layout studies, which includes need to locate a plan, influencing factors for plant location and evaluation of location alternatives. Chapter 2 presents plant layout, which discusses types of production systems, mass production system, principles of layout and types of layout. It is followed by a chapter on line balancing, which includes topics on frame of assembly line, types of assemble line, rank positional weight method for single model assembly line balancing and introduction to mixed model assembly line balancing.

Chapter 4 presents role of material handling, types of material handling, automated material handling, principles of material handling, factors influencing the selection of material handling equipment and types of material handling equipment. Next, Chapter 5 is on work study, which includes method study, and work measurement techniques. The method study presents different recording techniques, charts and principle of motion economy. The work measurement includes time study, work sampling and predetermined motion time system (PMTS). The next chapter is on production planning and control, which presents functions of production planning and control, materials management, inventory control and production scheduling.

Following this chapter, the chapter 7 presents quality control, which includes control charts and acceptance sampling plan. Chapter 8 presents management concepts with detailed focus on nature of management, levels of management, functions of management, and contribution of F.W Taylor and Hendry Fayol to theories of management. Chapter 9 presents need for financial planning, objectives of financial planning, functions of financial management, evaluation of alternatives and break-even analysis. The next chapter 10 is on marketing management, which focusses on marketing philosophy, pricing, channels of distribution, advertising, market research, and SWOT analysis. At the end, human resource management is presented which addresses objectives of human resource management, roles of human resource management, nature of human resource management, scope of human resource management, Maslow's hierarchy of needs, job analysis, job evaluation and management by objectives (MBO).

This text is written in easy-to-read style with lot of illustrations to explain the concepts with suitable techniques. Each chapter contains review questions at its end. The author expresses his sincere thanks to all his academic colleagues within his institute and in other institutions   for their encouraging support while writing this text. The author sincerely thanks Amazon for their support in providing a platform to publish this book.

P. Sivasankaran, M.E., Ph.D

CHAPTER 1 PLANT LOCATION STUDIES

1.1 INTRODUCTION

The term "plant location" describes the region and specific site chosen for the construction of a factory or business. However, the decision is only made after weighing the costs and advantages of other substitute sites. Once made, it is a strategic choice that cannot be reversed. The location should be chosen based on its unique requirements and conditions, and only if it can be changed without suffering a significant loss. Every single plant is a unique scenario in and of itself. A businessman should make an effort to choose the best or ideal location.

1.2 THE NEED TO LOCATE THE PLANT

There are various reasons to investigate the plant location problem. Three situations—which are listed below—lead to the requirement for choosing an appropriate location.

i. When establishing a new business
ii. The organization's current location preference
iii. In the event of a global location

1.2.1 When Establishing New Business

In the Beginning of a new organization, cost-savings are usually crucial while choosing a site for the first time or for new organization, but one should also consider the cost of long-term business/organizational goals. When choosing a location for new organizations, the following things should be taken into account.

i. Regional identification

The organizational goals and a variety of long-term factors, including marketing, technology, organizational internal strengths and weaknesses, region-specific resources and business environments, legal-governmental environments, social environments, and geographical environments, suggest a suitable region for the operations facility's location.

ii. Selecting a location inside a region

The next stage is selecting the ideal site when the appropriate region has been located.

iii.   Dimensional analysis

If all the costs were tangible and quantifiable, the comparison and selection of a site is easy. The location with the least cost is selected for implementation.

1.2.2 Organization's Current Location Preference

A manufacturing facility must thus integrate into a multi-plant operations strategy. In other words, more plant locations both on the same property and elsewhere under the ensuing conditions should focus on the following.

i.   Plants that produce specialized goods
ii.   Manufacturing plants supplying to a specific market area
iii.   Plants divided on the basis of the process or stages in manufacturing
iv.   Plants that emphasize adaptability

Plants that produce specialized goods

For the company, each factory provides services for the entire market area. When the demands for technology and resource inputs are specialized or noticeably different for the various product-lines, this technique is required, which means that a careful selection should be used while selecting plants that produce specialized goods.

Manufacturing plants s u p p l y i n g to a specific market area

Nearly all of the products the business produces are made at each of these plants. When market proximity concerns outweigh resource and technological concerns, this kind of strategy is advantageous. The corporate office must coordinate closely with this plan. Soft drink bottling factories are a blatant illustration of this tactic.

Plants divided on the basis of the process or stages in manufacturing

The equipment requirements, labor requirements, technological requirements, managerial policies, and managerial priorities may vary significantly depending on the production process or stage of manufacture. Since the output of one plant feeds into the input of the other, this strategy necessitates intensive centralization of manufacturing activity coordination by the corporate office, which must be aware of the numerous technological facets of all the plants.

Plants that emphasize adaptability

In order to satisfy the changing needs and simultaneously assure optimal use of the facilities and resources, this calls for extensive coordination between plants. It is not good for the company to frequently alter its long-term plan in an effort to temporarily increase its effectiveness. The key consideration in any facility site issue is whether the company can sustain its competitiveness in this area over the long term.

1.2.3   In the Event of Global Location

Globalization has caused Indian businesses to expand their operations abroad and foreign enterprises to establish offices in India. There is room for virtual proximity and virtual factories in the case of worldwide locations.

Virtual Nearness

With the development of telecommunications technology, a company can virtually be close to its clients. A large portion of the logistics for a software services company is carried out through information and communication. Several businesses execute a significant amount of their commercial interactions on the communications highway.

Online factory

In both the service and industrial sectors, many American and British companies frequently outsource parts of their company operations to countries like India. Consequently, a company could employ the operations facilities of its business partners instead of its own.

1.3 INFLUENCING FACTORS FOR PLANT LOCATION

The following are the various factors, which influence the plant location selection.

i.   Availability of Raw Materials

The availability of necessary raw materials has been one of the most crucial factors in choosing an industrial location. The primary benefit of having access to raw materials close to where the industry is located is that it saves money on shipping expenses.

ii.   Proximity to Market

Consumption is the best indicator of production. Without consumption, production has no value at all. Market activity, or selling commodities and products to consumers, is a component of consumption. As a result, no industry can be imagined without a market.

As a result, when considering the market, an entrepreneur must also examine prospective expansion, new territories, and the locations of competitors in addition to the existing category and the region.

iii.   Infrastructural Facilities

The location of an industry is determined by the availability of infrastructure facilities, which include power, transportation and communication, water, banking and other infrastructure.

iv.   Government Policy

The government also provides many incentives, concessions, tax breaks for a number of years, cheaper electricity supply, industrial shed, etc., to entice business owners to establish businesses in less developed and backward areas in order to promote the balanced regional development.

v.   **Availability of Manpower**

A further determining factor for the placement of skill intensive industries may be the availability of the necessary labor specialized in particular trades. The presence of technical training facilities in the region is beneficial when it comes to the availability of skilled employees.

vi.   **Ecological and Environmental Factors**

When determining where to locate a business, ecological and environmental problems like air and water pollution might be detrimental in some businesses. For instance, in addition to producing solid wate, manufacturing facilities can also damage the air and water.

Furthermore, strict waste disposal regulations, which apply to these businesses, drive up the cost of production to absurd levels.

Because of this, industries that could harm the ecosystem and environment of a region won't be built there. Entrepreneurs will not be allowed by the government to set up such companies in such ecologically and environmentally sensitive areas.

vii.   **Competition**

The location nearby plays a key role in choosing an enterprise's location in cases like retail stores where the revenue of a specific site depends on the level of competition from other competitors. The establishment of new units will not take place in locations where there is greater industry competitiveness. On the other side, new businesses tend to be founded in areas where there is either no or very little competition.

1.4 EVALUATING LOCATION ALTERNATIVES

The steps of location decision making procedure are listed below.

1. Decide on the criteria to use for evaluating location alternatives.
2. Identify important factors.
3. Develop location alternatives:
   a. Identify a general region for a location.
   b. Identify a small number of community alternatives.
   c. Identify site alternatives among the community alternatives.
4. Evaluate the alternatives and make a decision to select the site to build the plant/ business.

1.4.1 Locational Analysis

The plant location decision can be made using total cost curves of the potential locations. The components of this analysis are as given below.

- Level or volume of activity
- Unit selling price in each potential location
- Variable cost per unit in each potential location
- Total fixed cost in each potential location

The assumptions of the graph that is used in the location analysis graph are listed below.

1. Fixed cost is constant for the range of probable output.
2. Variable cost is linear for the range of probable output.
3. The required level of output can be closely estimated.
4. Only one product is involved in the analysis.

A sample graph with the total cost and volume for plant location selection is shown in Fig.1.1, which contains the total cost curves for three different locations, viz. A, B and C as functions of production quantity.

The formula for the total cost for each location is given by the following formula.

$$TC = FC + v \times Q$$

where,

TC is the total cost of the location

FC is the fixed cost

v is the variable cost per unit of production

Q is the quantity of production per period say year.

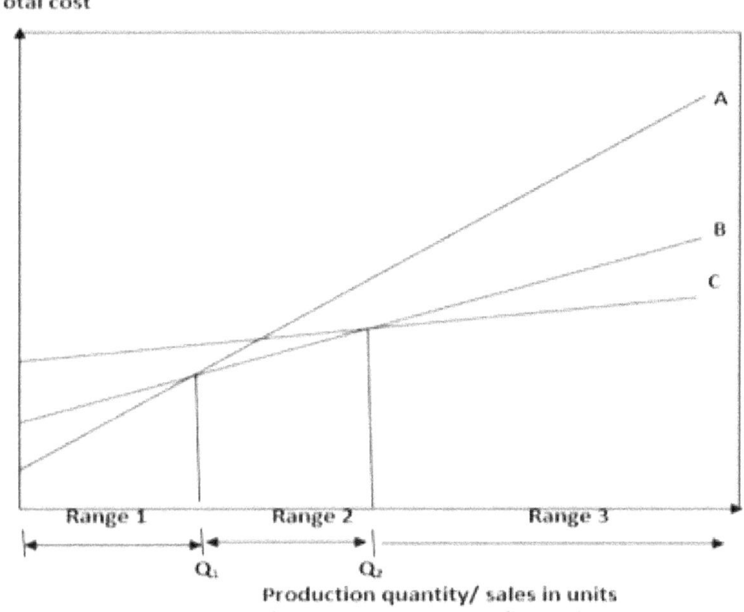

Fig.1.1 Graph of location analysis for best site selection

In the Fig.1.1,

if the production volume/ demand is less than Q_1, then the Site A is the best site,

if the production volume/ demand is in between Q_1 and Q_2, then the Site B is the best site

and

if the production volume/ demand is ,ore than Q_2, the the Site C is the best site.

1.4.2 Transportation Model for Distribution Planning

For distribution planning of a predetermined set of facilities and markets, a transportation model is a useful tool. Finding the most affordable method of transferring inventories of products or supplies from various origins to various locations where there is a demand for the commodities is the goal of the transportation problem. The nature of a transportation issue in the real world is depicted in Fig.1.2.

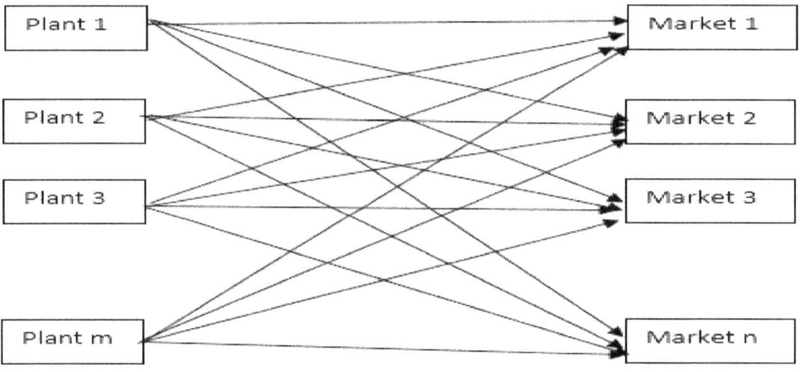

Fig.1.2 Transportation model framework

Below is a list of the data that this transportation model requires.

1. A list of sources (plants) along with their supply rates or capacities.

2. A list of market locations, along with information on their demands.

3. The average cost per item to ship between each origin and each destination

The following is a list of the model's presumptions.

1. The shipped goods are uniform.
2. The cost of shipping each individual product is the same, regardless of the quantity shipped.
3. Each origin and each destination are connected by a single route.

Applications of Transportation Model

Some potential applications of transportation model are as listed below.

• It is applied to supply chain management in logistics.

• It helps to have balanced supply and demand.

• It benefits to minimize the cost of shipping goods from sources to destinations.

REVIEW QUESTIONS

1. Define plant location.
2. Discuss the need for plant location study.
3. Discuss the influencing factors for plant location.
4. List the steps of evaluating plant location alternatives.
5. Illustrate the plant location analysis using a suitable graph.
6. Discuss the transportation model for distribution planning for a preset combination of plants and markets.

CHAPTER 2 PLANT LAYOUT

2.1 INTRODUCTION

An engineering study called a "plant layout study" is performed to evaluate various physical arrangements for a manufacturing facility. Facilities Planning and Layout is another name for it. The success of any manufacturing firm depends increasingly on their capacity to create and run manufacturing facilities that can swiftly and successfully adjust to shifting market and technological demands. Modern industrial facilities' primary foundation is now their plant layout design, which might affect some aspects of work efficiency. To design the most efficient plant architecture, it is necessary to properly arrange and position workers, materials, machinery, equipment, and other industrial supports and facilities.

2.2 TYPES OF PRODUCTION SYSTEMS

The production system is classified into the following types.

i. Job production system
ii. Batch production system
iii. Mass production system

2.2.1 Job Production System

A schematic view of job production is shown in Fig.2.1.

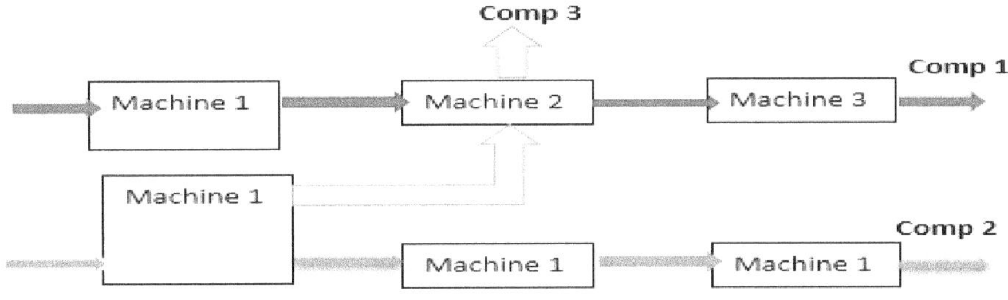

2.1 Schematic view of job production system

The following traits describe the job production system.

- There is a need for several general-purpose machines.
- There will need for a huge workforce with experience in many jobs.
- There may be minor production variances.
- Due to shifts in work load, some financial flexibility is necessary.
- A sizable supply of components, tools, and materials will be needed
- To meet the needs of manufacturing, the settings of the machines and equipment must be changed.
- Materials are intermittently moved through the process.

Limitations

The job production system's limitations are detailed below.

- Because production is done in small runs, it may not be possible to achieve the economies of large-scale production.
- The demand for some products fluctuates.
- The utilisation of labour and machinery could be ineffective.
- It is challenging to evaluate expenses scientifically.

2.2.2 Batch Production System

With the exception of manufacturing volume, this method is often comparable to job production. A batch or collection of products are produced all at once rather than just one product, as in the case with job production.

The batch production approach has the following features.
- The task is monotonous in nature.
- The functional arrangement of several production processes is included.
- One operation is completed on the entire batch before moving on to the next operation.
- Similar machines are grouped together in one location.
- It is typically used in industries with seasonal trade or there is a need to produce great variety of goods.

An illustrative batch production system is shown in Fig.2.2.

Advantages of Batch Production

The following list includes the batch manufacturing system's benefits.

- Batch systems handle repetitive tasks quickly and without requiring user input.
- Large organizations profit the most from it, although smaller firms can also use it.
- The sharing of the batch system across numerous users.
- The batch system has very little downtime.

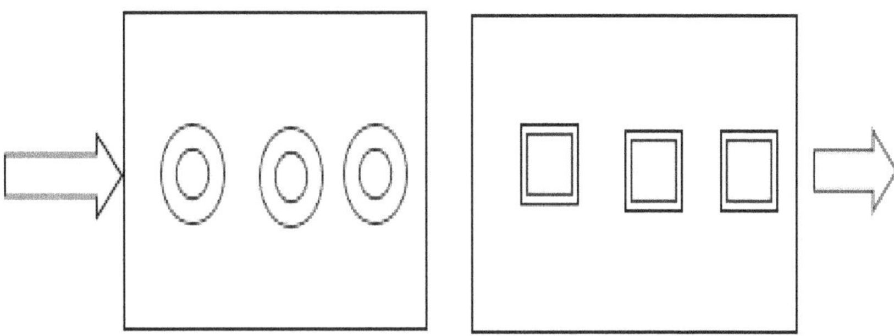

Limitations of Batch Production

Some major limitations of the batch production system are as listed below.

- Batch system usage requires training for computer operators.
- Batch systems are tough to debug.
- Batch systems can be expensive.
- When a task takes too long. i.e., if the machine of a job fails, other jobs will be delayed for an indeterminate period of time.

Below are a few illustrations of batch manufacturing methods.

- Reorder Level system
    In raw materials stores, at the end of every day, items will be reordered for the items for which the stock-on-hand went below its reorder level on that day.

- GPF Account Statement
    At the end of very financial year, the finance department of the organization will send GPF account statement to each employee.

2.3 MASS PRODUCTION SYSTEM

A mass production system entails the large-scale, continuous production of standardized goods. Production continues using this technology in anticipation of future demand. Mass production is built on standardization.

2.3.1 Characteristics of Mass Production System

The characteristics of the mass production system are as listed below.

- The units will flow from one operation point to the next.
- The items, equipment, supplies, and techniques are similar.
- There will be a specific machine for each operation.
- Production is carried out in advance of demand.
- The rate of production is often high.
- Machine configurations stay the same for a sizably long time.
- Any production flow error must be fixed right away to prevent a complete production stoppage.

2.3.2 Advantages of Mass Production

The mass production system has the following major advantages.
- Specialized labor results in a higher productivity and higher-quality product.
- Due to its substantial customs, a major corporation can obtain better conditions when purchasing raw materials and other accessories.
- The unit cost of production will be less when compared to the batch production system.

2.3.3 Disadvantages of Mass Production

The following is a list of the drawbacks of the mass production system.

- A large-scale producer is unable to focus entirely.
- Overproduction could occur with large-scale production.
- Facility utilization may be less when compared to the batch production system.

An overview of the mass production system is shown in Fig.2.3.

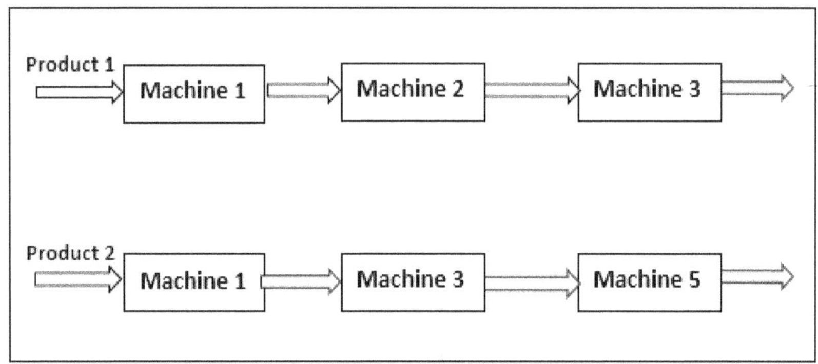

Fig.2.3 Overview of mass production system

2.4 PRINCIPLES OF LAYOUT

The principles of layout are listed below.

i. Overall integration
ii. Minimum distance
iii. Flow of materails
iv. Cubic space utilization
v. Satisfaction and safety
vi. Fexibility

Principle of Overall Integration

This principle states that the ideal layout is one that offers tasks and any other similar elements that lead to the best integration of production facilities like labour, machinery, and raw materials.

Principle of Minimum Distance

According to this principle, the movements of men and materials should be minimized.

Principle of Flow of Materials

The optimal plan of the flow is one in which the work stations are arranged in the same order or sequence that the materials are assembled.

Principle of Cubic Space Utilization

This means that the optimum arrangement makes efficient use of cubic space, i.e., space that is available in both vertical and horizontal directions.

Principle of Satisfaction and Safety

This rule states that the optimal plan is one that offers all workers satisfaction and safety.

Principle of Flexibility

The flexibility principle enables adoption and rearrangements at the lowest possible cost and with the least difficulty in the automotive and other related industries where product models vary over time.

2.5 TYPES OF LAYOUTS

The different types of the layout are as given below.
- Process layout/ Functional layout
- Product layout/ Line layout
- Group technology layout
- Fixed position layout

2.5.1 Process Layout/ Functional Layout

The machines are grouped in this type of architecture based on the nature or type of the operations rather than the order of the actions. Fig. 2.4 displays a line diagram of the process configuration.

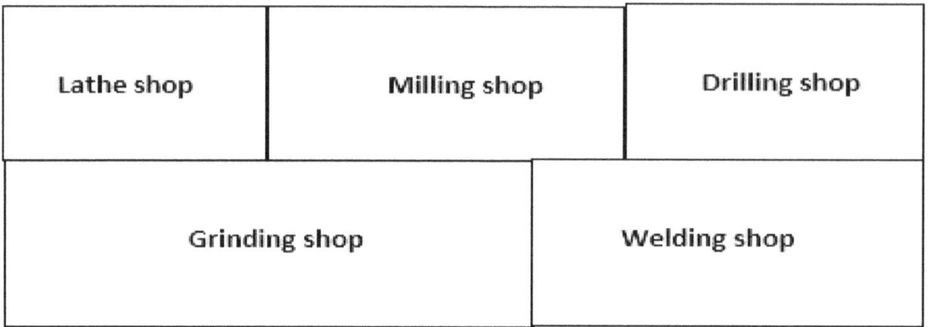

Fig.2.4 Line diagram of process layout

The following is a list of the benefits of the process layout.

- There is greater flexibility in the equipment and human resources, which makes load distribution simple.
- It enables better and more efficient monitoring through specialization at various levels.
- Work can be moved to another machine or work location to handle machine failure.

The following is a list of the process layout's drawbacks.

- Longer product flow durations due to intermittent flow of materials and greater number of machine setups.
- Production planning and management are more difficult, and a lot of paperwork is required.
- To finish all aspects of the job, workers must have excellent sill levels.

2.5.2 Product Layout/ Line Layout

This layout is referred to as a product kind of layout if every piece of processing machinery and equipment is set up in accordance with the order of the product's operations. Fig. 2.5 depicts a schematic illustration of the product arrangement.

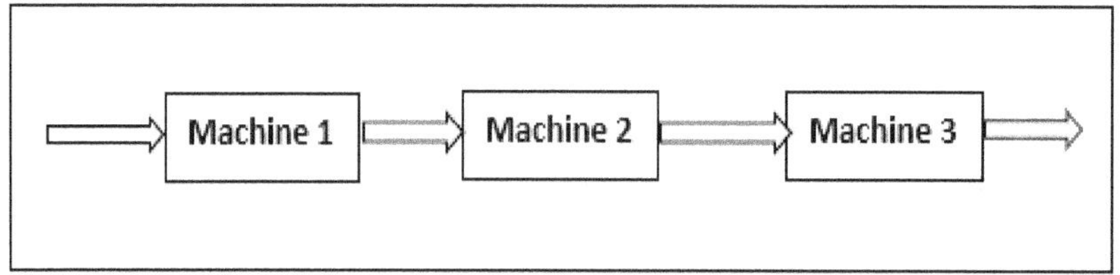

Fig.2.5 Product layout/ Line layout

Advantages offered by Product Layout

The advantages of the product layout are as listed below.

- It results in fewer work-in-progress and lowers overall material handling costs.
- It ensures greater utilization of both people and machines.
- This layout uses less floor space for temporary storage and items in transit.
- It makes production control more straightforward, which means that the cost of material handling will be very minimal.
- It cuts down on overall production time

Disadvantages of Product Layout

The disadvantages of the product layout are listed below.

- For this configuration, a larger maintenance crew is required.
- This arrangement uses extremely few different jobs, which lowers job satisfaction and increases worker boredom.

2.5.3 Group Technology Layout

The advantages of the process layout and the product layout—low equipment investment costs in the process layout and lower handling costs in the product layout—are combined in the group technology layout. Fig. 2.6 displays a schematic representation of the group's technological setup. In this layout, the components and machines are clustered based on similarity among them with the objective of minimizing intercell (inter group) movements.

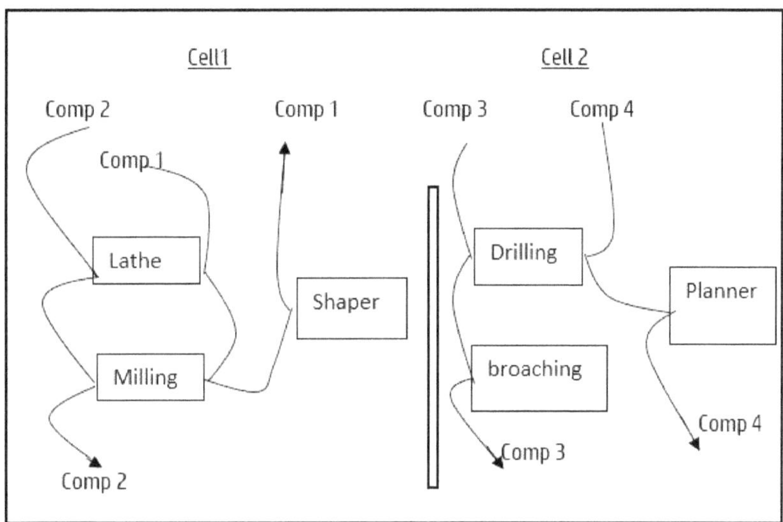

Fig.2.6 Schematic view of group technology layout

Advantages of Group Technology Layout

The group technology layout results with the following advantages.

- Reduced materials handling cost is assured.

- Increased equipment utilization is a reality.
- In-process inventory is moderate in this system of layout.
- Production control is very simple in this system of layout.

Disadvantages of Group Technology Layout

This system of layout has all advantages provided by the process layout and product layout, if there are similarities among the process sequences of the components; otherwise, the drawbacks of process layout and product layout will prevail.

2.5.4   Fixed Position Layout

The manufacturing industries of today place the least importance on this type of arrangement. The primary component of this sort of layout is fixed in place, and additional materials, parts, tools, machines, labor, and other supporting equipment are carried to this site. Fig. 2.7 displays a schematic representation of the fixed position layout.

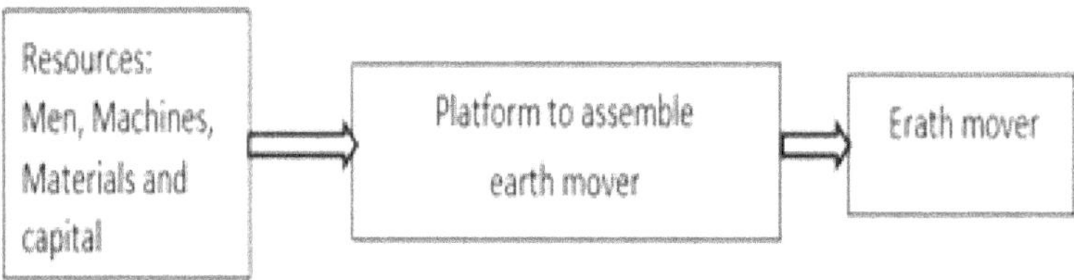

Fig.2.7 Fixed position layout

Advantages Offered by Fixed Position Layout

- Because a group of operators typically completes the work, operations are guaranteed to continue.
- There is less shifting of materials.
- Production facilities operate apart from one another. As a result, planning and loading may be done effectively. This will lower the overall cost of production.

Disadvantages of Fixed Position Layout

The following is a summary of the drawbacks of the fixed position arrangement.
- The work area for many fixed-position layouts may be cramped, leaving little room for storage.
- The fixed-position layouts have a greater administrative load, which can lead to issues with material handling.
- The range of control may be limited, and coordination may be challenging.

REVIEW QUESTIONS

1. Define plant layout.
2. What are the types of production system? Explain them with their advantages and disadvantages.
3. What is job production system? List its limitations.
4. What is batch production system? List its advantages and disadvantages.
5. What is mass production system? List its advantages and disadvantages.
6. Discuss the principles of layout.
7. What are the types of layouts? Explain them in brief.
8. What is process layout? Discuss its advantages and disadvantages.
9. What is product layout? Discuss its advantages and disadvantages.
10. What is group technology layout? Discuss its advantages.
11. What is fixed position layout? Discuss its advantages and disadvantages.

CHAPTER 3 LINE BALANCING

3.1 INTRODUCTION

Production strategy that involves setting an intended rate of production for required materials to be fabricated within a particular time frame is of more importance. In addition, effective line balancing requires assuring that every line segment's production quota can be met within the time frame using the available production. The objective of the line balancing problem is to group the tasks of assembling product into a minimum number of workstations subject to cycle time and task precedence constraints. A macro view of an assembly line in operation is shown in Fig.3.1.

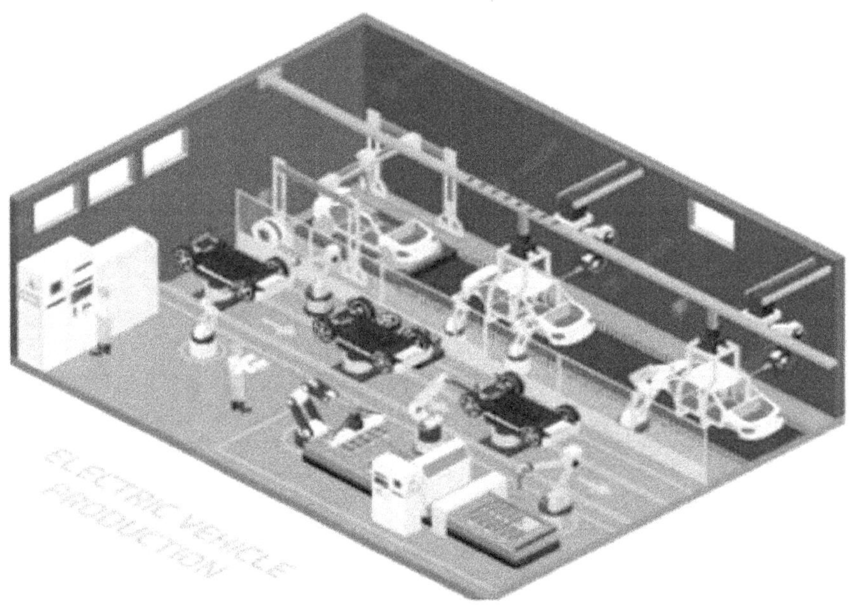

Fig.3.1 Macro view of assembly line in operation

3.2 FRAMEWORK OF ASSEMBLY LINE

The assembly line is classified into three types as listed below.
    i. Manual Single-Station Assembly

ii. Manual Assembly Lines

iii.　　Automated assembly line

3.2.1　Manual Single-Station Assembly Line

The following is a definition of the manual single-station assembly line.

• Have a single location where the product or a significant portion of its subassembly is completed.

• Depending on the size of the product and the production rate, one or more workers may be used on a complex product that is produced in small numbers. such as industrial machinery, aircraft, ships, and sophisticated consumer goods (appliances, car.).

The layout of a sample manual single-station assembly line is shown in Fig.3.2, which follows fixed position layout.

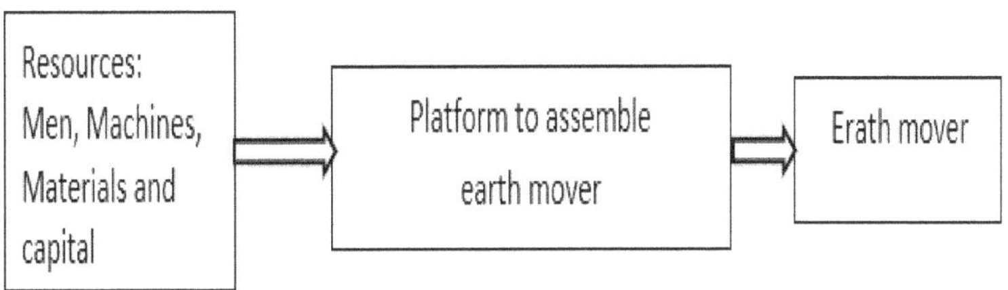

Fig3.2 Layout of manual single- station assembly

3.2.2　Manual Assembly Line

Product (subassembly) is passed from station to station along the line, where the assembly job is completed at various workstations. By adding one or more components to the existing subassembly, one or more human workers at each workstation complete a portion of the product's entire assembly task. Fig.3.3 depicts the design of a sample manual assembly line.

3.2.3　Automated Assembly System

The automated assembly line is identical to the manual assembly line, except robots or other automated devices work in place of the operators.

Fig.3.4 depicts the assembly line's layout, which employs robots at every workstation of the assembly line.

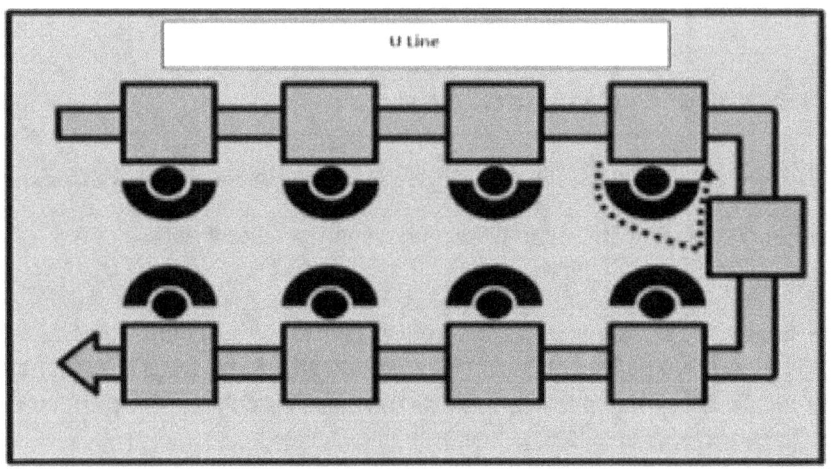

Fig.3.3 Layout of manual assembly lines

Fig 3.4 Layout of automated assembly system

3.3 TYPES OF ASSEMBLY LINE

The assembly line has two types as listed below.

I, Single model assembly line
ii. Mixed model assembly line

3.3.1   Single Model Assembly Line

Mass production gives the advantage of reduced setup times and improved production volume of a product. Industries follow line layout for the mass production system. In auto industry, engine production involves the assembly of different components, viz. crankcase, cylinder, head, connecting rod, piston, valves, cam, silencer, different bearings, etc. as per a given precedence assembly sequence. This assembly process involves manual operations. This is an example of line balancing problem in which the objective is to group the tasks of assembling the product into a minimum number of workstations without violating the precedence relationships as well as the cycle time constraint such that the balancing efficiency of the assembly line is maximized.

The following is a list of the inputs to the assembly line balance problem.
* Precedence network of tasks along with their timings
* Production volume per shift of the product

Fig.3.5 depicts a sample precedence network of a product's parts. In Fig.3.5, the time of each component is entered at the top of the corresponding node of the assembly network, and a component number is entered within the circle/node of the assembly network at each node. The Activities ON Nodes (AON) diagram is the name of this network.

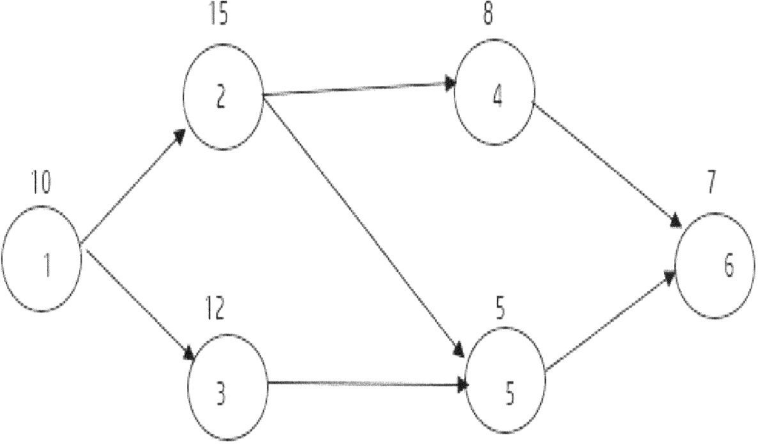

Fig.3.5 Precedence diagram of product

The cycle time is the total time (Maximum time) that is allotted to each workstation as given by the following formula.

$$Cycle\ time = \frac{Total\ time\ available\ per\ shift}{Production\ volume\ per\ shift}$$

The balancing efficiency of the solution of the line balancing problem is given by the following formula

$$Balancing\ efficiency\ in\ percentage$$
$$= \frac{Sum\ of\ the\ times\ of\ all\ components\ of\ the\ product}{Number\ of\ workstations \times Cycle\ time} \times 100$$

$$= \left(\frac{\sum_{i=1}^{n} t_i}{N \times CT}\right) \times 100$$

where,

n is the number of tasks
t_i is the required time of the task i
CT is the cycle time
N is the number of workstations

In the literature, this topic is frequently referred to as the SALBP-1 problem if the goal is to reduce the number of workstations for a fixed production rate. Fig.3.6 depicts a sample single model assembly line implementation.

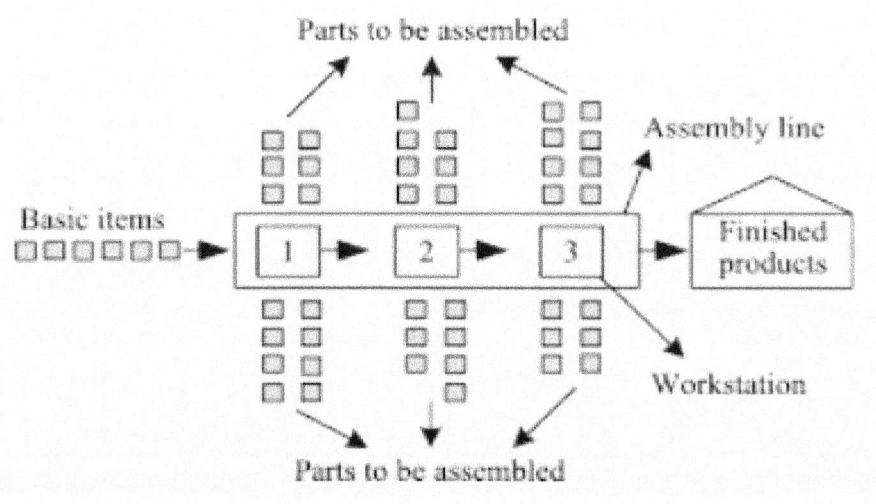

Fig 3.6 Single Model Assembly line system

3..3.1.1 Rank Positional Weight Method for Single Model Assembly Line

The steps of the Rank Positional Weight Method are presented below.

Step1: Draw the precedence diagram of the operations of the product that is to be assembled.

Step 2: For each operation, determine its positional weight. It is the total time all the succeeding components from that operation plus the duration of that operation.

Step 3: Rank the operations in descending order of ranked positional weight (R.P.W).

Step 4: Assign the operation to a station.

    Step 4.1 Form List A which consist of operations for which the following two conditions are satisfied.

    For each operation,

    i. All its immediate predecessors are already assigned if they are present or if there is no preceding operation.

    ii. The time of the operation is less than or equal to the cycle time.

    Step.4.2 Choose the operation with the highest RPW from the List A.

    Step 4.3 Assign that operation to current workstation and perform the following.

    i. Change all its immediate predecessors in the data matrix to 0.

    ii. Delete the row in the data table corresponding to the that operation.

    Step 4.4 Repeat Step 4.1 to Step 4.3 till it is not possible to assign any more operation to the current workstation.

Step 5: Repeat the Step 4 till all the operations are assigned to minimum number of workstations.

After designing the assembly line, its efficiency is computed using the following formula, which is called as balancing efficiency.

$$Balancing\ efficiency\ in\ percentage = \frac{Sum\ of\ the\ times\ of\ all\ components\ of\ the\ product}{Number\ of\ workstations \times Cycle\ time} \times 100$$

The idle time of a workstation is defined as the difference between the cycle time and the total of the times of the components assigned to it. By reducing the number of workstations on the assembly line, it is possible to achieve the goal of minimizing the workstations' total idle times.

Example 3.1

Consider the assembly network relationships of a product as given in Table 3.1. The number of shifts per day is one and the number of working hours per shift is 8. The company aims to produce 40 units of the product per day. Group the activities into workstations using Rank Positional Weight Method and compute balancing efficiency.

Table 3.1 Assembly Network Relationships with Times

Operation number	Immediate Preceding task(s)	Duration (minutes)
1	–	7
2	1	2
3	1	2
4	1	5
5	2, 3	8
6	3, 4	3
7	5	4
8	5, 6	7
9	4, 6	9
10	7, 8, 9	8

Solution.

a) Number of shifts per day = 1
Working hours per shift = 8 hours
Production volume per shift = 40 units

$$Cycle\ time = \frac{Total\ time\ available\ per\ shift}{Production\ volume\ per\ shift} = \frac{8 \times 60}{40} = 12\ minutes$$

The summary of data of the given problem is in Table 3.2. The design of workstations can be seen in Table 3.3.

Table 3.2 Summary of Data of the Given Problem

Operation number	Duration (minutes)	Positional weight (Min)	Immediate predecessor(s)		
1	7	55	0	0	0
2	2	29	1	0	0
3	2	41	1	0	0
4	5	32	1	0	0
5	8	27	2	3	0
6	3	27	3	4	0
7	4	12	5	0	0
8	7	15	5	6	0
9	9	17	4	6	0
10	8	8	7	8	9

Table 3.3 Design of Workstations

Station Number	List A	Operation	Unassigned Cycle Time (UACT)
I	–	–	12
	1	1	5
	2, 3, 4	3	3
	2	2	1
II	–	–	12
	4, 5	4	7
	6	6	4
III	–	–	12
	5, 9	5	4
	7	7	0
IV	–	–	12
	8, 9	9	3
V	–	–	12
	8	8	5
VI	–	–	12
	10	10	4

$$Balancing\ efficiency\ in\ percentage = \frac{Sum\ of\ the\ times\ of\ all\ components\ of\ the\ product}{Number\ of\ workstations \times Cycle\ time} \times 100$$

$$= \frac{55}{6 \times 12} \times 100 = 76.39\%$$

3.3.2 MIXED MODEL ASSEMBLY LINE BALANCING

There are two main categories for the assembly line balance problem: ALBP 1 and ALBP 2. The ALBP 1 is a type 1 assembly line balancing problem in which the goal is to divide the tasks among the fewest possible workstations for a specific cycle time, hence increasing the assembly line's balancing efficiency. The ALBP 2 is a type 2 assembly line balancing issue in which the jobs are distributed among a predetermined number of workstations in order to reduce the cycle time, which is the maximum of the task times for all of the workstations. This ultimately maximizes the rate of production.

Each model will have a cycle time in the mixed model assembly line balancing problem, as opposed to the single model assembly line balancing problem, where each model's cycle time is typically calculated based on the required production volume per shift of that model. In a scenario with two models, the cycle time is 20 minutes if Model 1's manufacturing volume is 24 assemblies each shift. Model 2 has a cycle time of 10 minutes when the production volume per shift is 48 assemblies. Each cycle time can be taken as it is in the case of a single model and not modified. The line may be built for a common cycle in the mixed-model assembly line balancing challenge.

Think about Models 1 and 2, whose respective precedence networks are displayed in Figs. 3.7 and 3.8. The task time is shown by the number next to each node. The combined model's precedence network, which comprises of the tasks from both models with merged precedence relationships, is shown in **Fig.3.9**. The tasks from each separate model are integrated to form the set of tasks in the combined model.

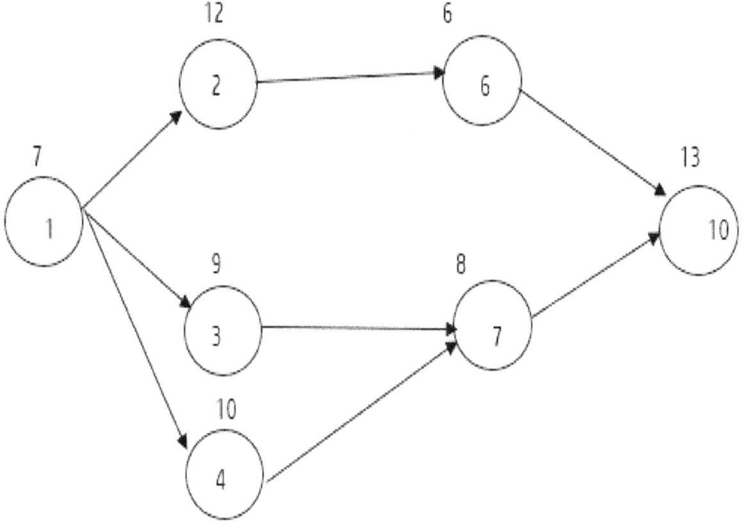

Fig.3.7 Precedence network of Model 1

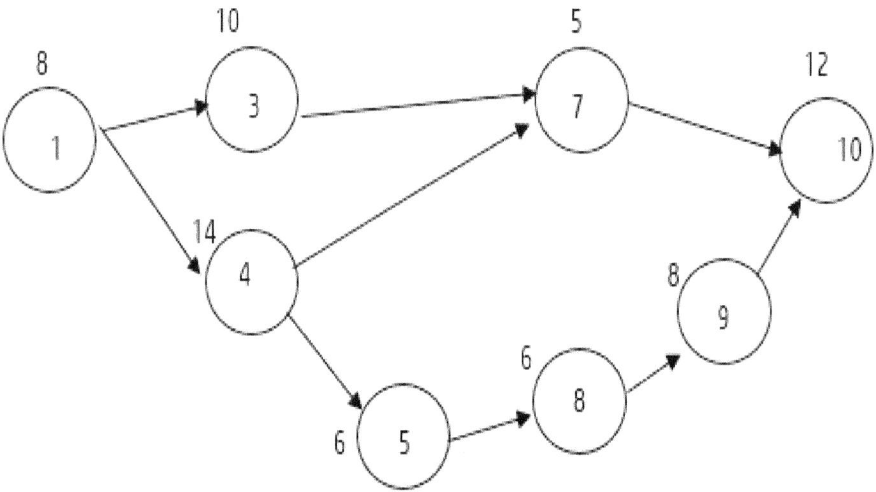

Fig.3.8 Precedence network of Model 2

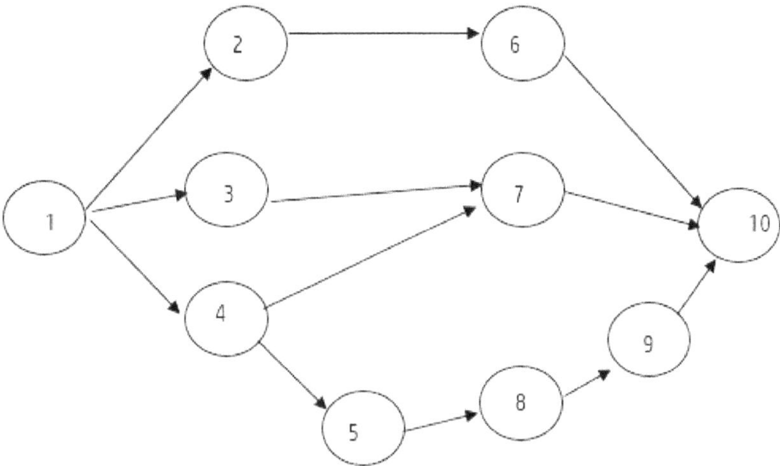

Fig.3.9 Combined model of Model 1 and Model 2

Researchers in the past computed average task time for each of the tasks in the combined model. But, in this work, the average task time is not computed. Instead, the original task times of the models are used as such in the design of the assembly line without any modification, because it introduces perfection in the design of the assembly line in terms of reduced number of workstations.

Mixed-model assembly line balancing is a reality in many organizations. The mixed-model assembly line balancing problem comes under combinatorial category. So, an attempt has been made to genetic algorithm for the mixed- model assembly line balancing problem such that the combined balancing efficiency is maximized, where the combined balancing efficiency is the average of the balancing efficiencies of the individual models (Sivasankaran (Sivasankaran and Shahabudeen, 2013).

3.3.2.1 PROBLEM STATEMENT

The mixed-model straight type assembly line balance problem, which has M models, is the issue under discussion in this work. The total set of tasks for the combined model is formed by adding the individual task sets from each model. In the combined model, there are n total tasks. Each model has a deterministic task time that corresponds to any tasks that are present. A task's time is presumed to be zero if it is not present in a model. The following formula is used to calculate the cycle time based on a specified production volume per shift.

$$Cycle\ Time\ (CT) = \frac{Effective\ Time\ avaialble\ per\ shift}{Production\ volume\ per\ shift}$$

The balancing efficiency of the solution of the line balancing problem is given by the following.

$$Balancing\ efficiency\quad = \left(\frac{Sum\ of\ all\ task\ times}{Number\ of\ workstations\ \times\ Cycle\ time}\right) \times 100$$

$$= \left(\frac{\sum_{j=1}^{n} t_j}{N \times CT}\right) \times 100$$

where,

n is the number of tasks

t_j is the required time of the task j

CT is the cycle time

N is the number of workstations

The *ALBP* 1 problem with a mixed-model is considered. In this problem, there will be many models which are to be produced in batches using the same assembly line. The presence of a mixed-model makes the design of the assembly line more complex, in terms of processing times of the tasks and cycle times of the model. The average processing time (T_j) of each task as given by the following formula is normally taken as the representative value of the task time for that task.

$$T_j = \frac{\sum_{i=1}^{M} t_{ij}}{NM_j}\ for\ j = 1, 2, 3, \ldots, n, whete\ t_{ij} \neq 0$$

where,

t_{ij} is the time of the task j in the model i

n is the number of tasks

M is the number of models

T_j is the average time of the task j

NM_j is the number of models in which the processing time of the task j is more than zero.

Instead of utilizing the average task times for the tasks in the combined model to construct the assembly lines, the original task times are used in this work.

The objective is to group the tasks of the combined model into a minimum number of workstations without violating precedence constraints for a common cycle time, which is derived based on the cycle times of the models. Generally, the common cycle time is the average of the cycle times of the models. In this work a genetic algorithm is designed for the mixed-model assembly line balancing problem, in which the original times of the tasks are used while concurrently designing the workstations of the models, such that the combined balancing efficiency is maximized. The combined balancing efficiency is the average of the balancing efficiencies of the models.

3.3.2.2 Construction of Ordered Vector

Utilizing a cross over strategy, a genetic algorithm based on the combined precedence network can tackle this issue. The population is made up of many chromosomes. Table 3.4 depicts a sample chromosome.

Table 3.4 Display of Sample Chromosome Made Up of Operations in Random Order.

Position	1	2	3	4	5	6	7	8	9	10
Chromosome 1	5	7	8	3	4	1	9	2	10	6

In the genetic algorithm to design the mixed model assembly line for maximizing the balancing average balancing efficiency, the tasks in the combined network of the models are put in random order to form a chromosome. If the tasks as the order of appearance in the chromosome are considered serially without any rearrangement of the tasks in the chromosome, the assignment of the tasks to different workstations may not be feasible, which means that the precedence constraints among the tasks may be violated. Hence, the tasks in the chromosome should be reordered to create a sequence of tasks in that chromosome which ensures feasibility in terms of precedence relationship among those tasks. This is achieved through creation of ordered vector.

The application of the steps of constructing an ordered vector to this chromosome gives an ordered vector 1-3-4-5-7-8-9-2-6-10.

3.3.2.3 Evaluation of Fitness Function of Chromosome

The fitness function of the genetic algorithm applied to the mixed model assumedly line balancing problem is the average balancing efficiency of the models of the mixed model assembly line balancing problem. The cycle time of the model 1as well as that of the model 2 shown in Fig.3.7 and Fig.3.8, respectively is assumed as 20 minutes. Hence, the cycle time of the combined model is also 20 minutes, which is the average of the cycle times of both the models. The fitness function of a chromosome 1, namely balancing efficiency is obtained by assigning the tasks serially from left to right from its ordered vector 1-3-4-5-7-8-9-2-6-10 into workstations for the given cycle time of 20 minutes of the combined model as shown in Table 3.5.

While assigning a task into a workstation, that task pertaining to all the models should be assigned to the same workstation. If a task is available in only one model, then that can be independently assigned to the current workstation.

Table 3.5 Solution and Fitness Function Value of Ordered Vector 1-3-4-5-7-8-9-2-6-10

Workstation	Assigned Tasks		Unassigned Times	
I	1	1	13	12
	3	3	4	2
II	4	4	10	6
	-	5	10	0
III	7	7	12	15
	-	8	12	9
	-	9	12	1
IV	2	-	8	20
	6	-	2	20
V	10	10	7	8
Balancing Efficiency			65%	86.25%
Combined Efficiency				75.63%

REVIEW QUESTIONS

1. What is assembly line balancing? State its objective.
2. Illustrate the manual single-station assembly line using a suitable sketch.
3. Illustrate manual assembly line balancing problem with a sketch.
4. Illustrate automated assembly line balancing problem with a sketch.
5. What is single model assembly line balancing problem? Explain its aspect and objective.
6. Distinguish between cycle time and balancing efficiency.
7. Give the steps of rank positional weight method applied to single model assembly line balancing problem.
8. Consider the assembly network relationships of a product as given in the following table. The number of shifts per day is one and the number of working hours per shift is 8. The company aims to produce 40 units of the product per day. Group the activities into workstations using Rank Positional Weight Method and compute balancing efficiency.

Assembly Network Relationships with Times

Operation number	Immediate Preceding task(s)	Duration (minutes)
1	–	9
2	1	2
3	1	4
4	1	5
5	2, 3	8
6	4	5
7	5	4
8	5, 6	5
9	4	9
10	7, 8, 9	7

9. What is mixed model assembly balancing problem? Illustrate the input data of this problem and the combined precedence network.
10. Illustrate the method of computing the balancing efficiency of a sample mixed model assembly line balancing problem for a given ordered vector with your own data.
11. Discuss the applications of the assembly line balancing problem in industries.

CHAPTER 4 MATERIAL HANDLING

4.1 INTRODUCTION

Material handling involves short-distance motions inside the shop floor of a company with the help of transportation vehicle to move materials and subassemblies from one place to another place. It makes use of an extensive variety of manual, semi-automated, and automatic device and consists of attention of the protection, storage, and control of substances in the course of their manufacturing, warehousing, distribution, consumption, and disposal. Material handling may be used to create time and place utility through the handling, storage, and control of material, as distinct from manufacturing, which creates shape utility through converting the shape and make-up of material.

The types of material handling are listed below.

- Production batch
- Transfer batch
- Unit load
- Single part

A schematic view of all the types is shown in Fig.4.1.

Production Batch: A production batch consists of a mix of components and subassemblies, which are moved through a production line while assembling a product. The movement of such batch is carried out by suitable material handling equipment, which pickups the batch from one machine and delivers to another machine in the production line. The selection of the material handling equipment plays a major role in minimizing the cost of handling.

Transfer Batch: Transfer batch consists of a bulk of components and subassemblies. Such batch is to be moved from one shop to another shop in a company or moved from one production center to another production center within the same shop. This requires specialized handling equipment with more handling capacity.

Unit Load: This means the maximum collection of homogenous parts from one location to another location such that the collection of the parts retains the original shape and size which prevailed at the time of loading them into a truck even after delivering the collection of parts at another location.

Single Part: Single part will be too heavy, which necessitates moving it in single piece from its existing location to a desired next location.

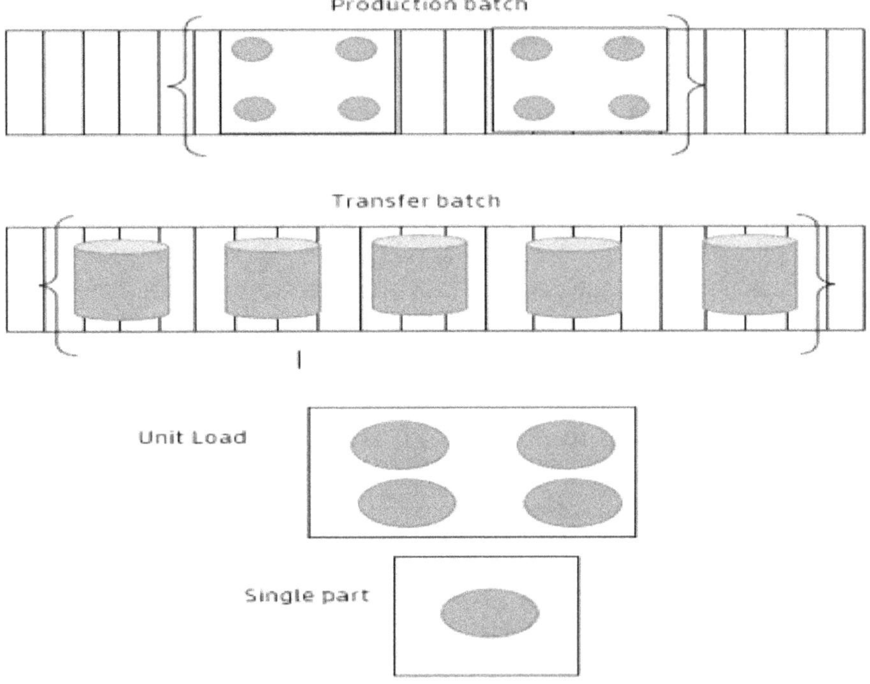

Fig4.1 Material Handling types

4.2 ROLE OF MATERIAL HANDLING

Material handling performs a vital function in manufacturing and logistics, which facilitates movement of every component and subassembly through conveyor or truck, overhead travelling cranes, etc. from a point of current processing to the next point of processing of those component and subassembly. The material handling activities can be seen in other applications such as movement of construction materials around the building that is constructed, moving containers into ships at harbor, etc. The productivity of a shop floor mainly depends on the efficiency and effectiveness of the material handling systems that are designed and implemented to handle the materials for their smooth flow aiming seamless integration of different subsystems of the shop.

Hence, the metrics of the material handling system are as listed below.

- Less throughput time/ cycle time of production of the product that is manufactured.
- Less damage to the components and subassemblies used in assembling a

product or machining a part.

- Quickly responding to pick up calls from work centers/ machines to load items from those work centers and then later to unload them in corresponding work centers.
- Avoidance of collision of one material handling equipment while it is in move with other material handling equipment.
- Appropriate selection of the material handling equipment to handle different materials in the shop floor.
- Use of automation in handling the materials.
- Use of automated guided vehicle system (AGVs) for timely pickups and deliveries of the components and subassemblies in the shop floor.
-

4.3 TYPES OF MATERIAL HANDLING

The material handling equipment are classified into the following categories based on extent of automation.

- Manual material handling system
- Automated material handling system
-

4.3.1 Manual Material Handling System

The manual material handling system uses low tech equipment that are operated by workers in the shop floor to move the components and subassemblies from one work place to another work place or from the raw material store to different production centers or from production centers to finished goods warehouse.

The hands and body members of the workers will be in more contact with the low-tech equipment for loading the components and subassemblies into trucks as well as unloading them from the trucks at other locations. Hence, it is the responsibility of the work-study engineer to design the man-machine system such that the anthropometrical measures of the workers match with man-machine system for better productivity. The manual material handling is mostly carried out using hand trolly, which is as shown in Fig.4.2.

Fig4.2 Hand Trolley

4.3.2 Merits of Manual Materials Handling System

The merits of the manual material handling system are as shown below.

i.   The cost of implementation of this system is low.
ii.   It has more flexibility in handling the materials in terms of variety and volume of handling.
iii.   It has more flexibility in handling the materials in terms of selecting travelling paths of material handling equipment in the shop floor from many possible travel paths.
iv.   It is possible to inbuild personal care towards handling of materials through proper instructions to workers and some safety devices in the handling equipment.

4.3.3 Demerits of Manual Material Handling System

The demerits of the manual materials handling systems are as listed below.

i.   This system of handling is not suitable for heavy components and subassemblies
ii.   Throughput time of the product will be more, which reduces the productivity of the company.
iii.   There will be delay in pickups of the components and subassemblies from machine centers.
iv.   This system may have more probability of injuries to workers.

4.4 AUTOMATED MATERIAL HANDLING SYSTEM

Most of the material handling equipment are semi-automated, which have their own merits and demerits. So, the use of automated material handling equipment in companies is a compulsion for better productivity. In companies, the shapes and sizes of the components that are moved from one place to another place may vary greatly. The use of sophisticated material handling equipment becomes essential while handing heavy objects as well as bulk materials subject to technical and economic feasibility of using such equipment.

Some of the automated material handling equipment are robots, equipment with sensors, conveyor, etc., which will fully automate the material handling tasks in companies.

A sample automated material handling system is shown in Fig.4.3, which is a conveyor that is used to move materials from one place to another place in the shop place. This is a material handling system between two fixed points. But it is very much useful for continues operation in the shop floor. Like this, there are many automated material handling devices, viz. transfer lines in factories, assembly conveyor to assemble two-wheeler or four-wheeler, etc. Further, more automation can be seen in electronic industries, food industries and in mines to transfer coal from mine bed to coal storage area at the ground level, etc.

Fig.4.3 Belt Coveyer

4.4.1 Merits of Automated Material Handling System

The merits of the automated material handling system as as listed below.

- It is used for bulk tranfer of materials
- It reduces the cycle time of production of products using production lines, which in turn increases the production volumes of the products that are assembled.
- This sytem avoids injuries to the employees.
- Increases the quality of the components, subassemblies and products manufactured in this system of manufacturing.

4.4.2 Demerits of Automated Material Handling System

The demerits of the automated material handling system are as listed below.

- The cost of implementing this system is high.
- Flexibility of volume of handling of materials is less.
- Flexibility of travel path of the handling equipment is very very less.
- Failure of auomated handling equipment will lead to complete stoppage of the production line, because this system of handling is used for production line/ transfer line.

4.5 PRINCIPLES OF MATERIAL HANDLING

The list of principles of material handling is given below.

i. Planning principle
ii. Standardization principle
iii. Work principle
iv. Ergonomic principle
v. Unit load principle
vi. Space utilization principle

vii.	System principle
viii.	Automation principle
ix.	Environmental principle
x.	Life cycle cost principle

Planning Principle: The methods that are used in converting the raw materisl into finished goods play a major role in terms of usgage of material handling system. Hence, there should be proper planning of the methods of manufacturing and their integration with appropriate material handling systems. This will minimize the cost of the material handling system and increase the productivity of the shop floor.

Standardization Principle: The components of the material handling system are equipment, controls and software, which must be stardardised to faciliate overall increase in the performance objectives such that the flexibility, modularity and production are not compromized. The standdardization of the equipment will facilitate easy maintenance of them and flexible schedule of handling equipment.

Work Principle: The material handling activity is a non-value adding activity. Hence, it must reduced to a greater extent to increase the productivity of the company. This requires an appropriate design of man-machine system as well as an efficinet shop floor layout.

Ergonomic Principle: The design of the material handling system should consider the ergonomic aspect of the labour force that is associated with such activities. Ergonomics is the study of anthropometric data of the employees, which msut be considered while deisgning the material handling system, which will increase the effectiveness of such system and inturn increase the productivity of the shop floor.

Unit Load Principle: The unit load principle decides the configuartion of the batch of materials to be handled in terms of shape and size. The shape and size of the material that is picked up from a location should retain its shape and size, when that material is delived in another location.

Space Utilization Principle: The extent of space that is used to convert the raw materials into finished products plays a major role in material handling activities. If the space used is lesser for a given volume of production, then the extent of material handling will be minimal. Further, the third dimension of the shop floor should be used. The deisgn of efficient layout of the shop floor facilitates effective space utilization.

System Principle: System is a collection of integrated elements. The manufacturing system consists of material receipt subsystem, storage system, production system, quality inspection system, finsihed goods storage system and packagiing. Every meaningful pair of subsystems need one or more material handling systems. So, the proper selection and implemenation of the material handling system should integrate all the subsystems of the company for better productivity.

Automation Principle: Automation is the key to improve the productivity of the shop floor in the long run. Though the cost of implementing the automated material handling system is more, it will be reduced to a greater extent in the long run and hence the productivity of the shop floor. Some of the examples of the automated material handling system are conveyor, transfer lines, Automated Guided Vehicle System (AGVS), roller conveyor, etc.

The bebefits of this principle are as listed below.

- Throughput time of the product that is assembled in a production line will be reduced. This will increase the production volume of the product per unit time.
- The labour cost associated with automated material handling system will be minimal.
- This system of handling instals consistency in maintaining quality of products manufactured in the system.
- This increases specialization among the workers.
- The auomated material handling system will reduce Industrial accidents to a minimal level.
- The workers will have more job satisfaction.

Environmental Principle: The materrail handling system consumes energy and also affect the impact on environment due to proloned storage of materials in the same place. So, the system must be designed such that the energy consumption as well as the impact of the operation of material handling system on the environment is reduced.

Life Cycle Cost principle: As already stated, the automated material handling system like AGVs will be costly. But, in the long run, there will be benefit of reduced manpower for material handling.

So, an economic analysis is to be carried out to compare the present system of material handling and the proposed automated system of material handling by taking the following costs of the automated system.

1. Purcahse cost (Plus value)
2. Annual maintentance cost (Plus value)
3. Life of the equipment
4. Salvage value at the end of the life (Plus value)
5. Savings due to decreased manpower (Minus value)

One should compute the annual equivalent cost of the proposed system, which must be compared with that of the present system of material handling. If the annaul equivalent cost of the auomated material handling system is less, then the company should buy that system of material handling and implement in the company.

4.6 FACTORS INFLUENCING SELECTION OF MATERIAL HANDLING EQUIPMENT

The selection of material handling equipment considers the following three important elements.

i.   Production problems/ tasks

ii.   The capabilities of the exiting material handling equipment

iii.   Human factors that are associated with the system of material handling

The selection of the material handling equipment should combine all the above elements such that the unit cost of handling is very minimal.

The factors that are to be considered while selecting a material handling equipment are listed below.

- **Adaptability:** The load carrying capacities and material movement characteristics of the material handling equipment should fit into the system of material handling.
- **Flexibility:** Though the initial assignments of the material handling equipment to different material handling tasks of the shop floor are done by intuition, on necessity they are flexible enough to reassign them to varied tasks, which are different from the originally assigned material handling tasks. This attribute leads to minimize the downtime of the machines of the shop floor.
- **Load carrying capacity:** The load carrying capacity of the material handling equipment should be designed such that it is sufficient enough to handle more tasks and at the same time one should remember the fact that over capacity leads to increased cost of such equipment.
- **Speed:** The fast movement of a material handling equipment will reduce the non-value adding component of the throughput time of the product that is manufactured in the shop floor. At the same time, the fast movement of the handling equipment may lead to unsafe operation and in turn to industrial accidents. Hence, a compromise should be arrived in the speed of the vehicle by taking the capacity and speed of the handling equipment into account.
- **Space requirements:** The selection of the material handling should be such that the total space required for the movement of them is minimal in the shop floor.
- **Level of Supervision**: The design of the material equipment should include the degree of automaticity in it, which means less supervision on that equipment, when it is in use.
- **Ease of maintenance:** The selection of a material handling equipment should aim to minimize the cost of maintenance of that equipment.
- **Environment:** The material handling equipment should facilitate less negative impact on environment and adhere to environmental regulations.
- **Cost:** The purchase cost of the material handling equipment should be

economical such that the unit cost of material handling is very minimal.

4.7 TYPES OF MATERIAL HANDLING EQUIPEMENT

The materials handling equipmet are classified into the following types.

i.   Bulk material handling equipment
ii.   Engineerd system
iii.   Industrail trucks
iv.   Storage and handling equipment

4.7.1   Bulk Material handling System

The forms of bulk materials are as listed below.

* Loose form
* Liquid form
* Food
* Metal items
* Minerals

The bulk material handling equipment are deisgned to transport, store and control bulk materials in industries. Some examples of bulk material handling equipment are hoopers, relaimers, conveyor belts, stackers, bucket and grain elevators, etc.

Hopper: This is a funnel shaped equipment, which opens and close. This is used to pour loose materials into containers.

Relaimer: This is a material handling device which is used to pickup materials in bulk form from a stockpile of a company.

Coveryer belt: A converyer belt is used to transfer materials in loose form from one location to another location. This is supported by roller/ drum at the start location and end location internally. The use of belt conveyor in mines to bring the coal from mines bed to earth surface, move coal from the stockyard of a thermal power station to its boiler, etc.

Stacker: These are bulk material handling equipment to tranfer loose materials into stockpile of a company on their own.

Bucket and Grain Elevators: These are used to move loose materials vertically upward to store materials. An example use of this is in rice mill to move paddy from stockyard to boiler, from there to drying unit and then to gringing unit.

4.7.2   Engineered Systems

The engineered systems are deisgned to handle bulk materials. The examples of the engineered systems are listed below.

* Automated storage and retrieval system (AD/RS)
* Automated guided vehicle system (AGVS)
* Robotic delivery system

- Conveyor system

Automated Storage and Retrieval System: This system uses shuttles for picking up loose materials and then placing them on designated parts of the system. The picking activity of this system can be manual or automated. This sytem can be connected to the company's network so that the movements of the materials and stocks can be monitoed by the associated managers.

Automated Guided Vehicles System (AGVS): Automated guided vehicle system is a computer controlled material handling vehicle to pickup material on demand from machine centers and deliver them at designated destination locations for further processing. They operate in a preset pathways.

Robotic Delivery System: Robots are used to deliver components and subassemblies at different stages of an assembly line from their preceeding stages of production, transfer hot billets from a furnace to forging machine for forging operation, etc.

Conveyor System: Conveyor system is used to transport materials from one place to another place through fixed path. The types of conveyor are mechanical conveyors, automotive conveyors, belt conveyor, belt-driven live roller conveyors, bucket conveyor, chain conveyor, chain-driven live roller conveyor, drag conveyor, etc.

REVIEW QUESTIONS

1. List and explain different types of material handling.
2. Discuss the role of material handling.
3. List and explain the types material handling based on the level of automation.
4. What is manual material handling system? Discuss its merits and demerits.
5. What is automated material handling system? Discuss its merits and demerits.
6. Discuss the principles of material handling.
7. List and explain the factors influencing the selection of material handling equipment.
8. Give the classification of material handling equipment with examples in each category.

CHAPTER 5 WORK STUDY

5.1 INTRODUCTION

Work study can increase a company's workplace efficiency. Method study and time study are both parts of the work study. The method study comes before the time study for a certain reality to refine the process. The time study will be used later to compute standard time.

5.2   METHOD STUDY

Method studies are essentially carried out to streamline processes and work toward greater productivity. It is always preferable to carry out the task with the intended outcome and the least amount of resource usage. A method describes how a task is to be completed. That is the description of how we consume resources in order to achieve our target.

As a result, the approaches can calculate how much input materials, labour, and money are used. Therefore, the use of appropriate methods may be seen as the core where one can try to reduce resource consumption thereby reducing cost per unit output. The cost and quality of the output produced are determined by the method that is designed and used.

5.2.1   Objectives of Method Study

The arrangement of machines and equipment, the flow of people and materials, and a broad inquiry and development of a shop or area are all topics of method study. Below is a list of the advantages of the method study.

- Process improvement as well as bettering the layout of the factory and workplace.
- An improvement in plant and equipment design.
- Reduction of movements and unneeded fatigue.
- Use of better tools, materials, and working conditions

5.2.2   Method Study Procedure

The steps of the method study procedure are as given below.

i.   Selection of the job
ii.   Recording the facts
iii. Critical examination of the facts
iv.   Development of new method
v.   Install the method
vi.   Maintain the method

Selection of the Job

The orientation and selection of objectives come first once the concept for a method study has been developed. The issue needs to be identified. The following is a summary of some typical issues that the Method Study investigator encounters and typically needs to resolve.

- Bottlenecks that prevent efficient material or process flow.
- Products that must be economically produced through the use of cost-cutting.
- Efficient use of space and including land.
- Economic use of labour and resources.
- Elimination of non-value-adding or idle time due to flow, queue, and other issues in the shop floor.

Recording the Facts

Before dismissing the current method or procedure, sufficient information regarding that current system must be gathered. This is done to make sure that a neutral record of how the work is done is kept. This record is based on the concerned investigator's direct observation in order to avoid the possibility of bias.

Critically Examine the Facts

This phase of the method study is crucial. The data being gathered is closely inspected, an d every aspect of the work is reviewed for the following.

- The component is completely removed.
- The component is coupled with another task-related component.
- The component is altered
- The component is condensed to reduce the amount of effort required to manufacture it.

Develop the New Method

New approach, layout, or procedure is developed using the options that were chosen. To evaluate their viability, these could need to go through test runs. If possible, it is desirable for testing of this sort to be conducted away from the work site. It is a good idea to involve departmental officers to help with challenges of new method acceptance in the department. The end result must be an improved method.

It must be well-liked by the workforce and departmental staff. It must adhere to all of their practical requirements and technical specifications.

Install the Method

The following must be decided before the new technique is installed.

- Any new part or supply that needs to be ordered;
- Potential adjustments to the production process
- Choosing the scope of the redeployment
- Establishing new documentation protocols
- Developing new test protocols and quality requirements
- A thorough schedule for implementing these changes

Maintaining the Method

A procedure that has been implemented usually changes gradually as a result of small adjustments made by the operators or supervisors. A reference standard (job instruction document) must be used as a comparison point in order to spot any changes. Similarly, a job specification—a document that corresponds to an incentive programme and includes information on the standard time for each job—is created.

5.2.3 Recording Techniques

After selecting the job for Method Study, the method study engineer should collect and record all the relevant data. The data of the existing method are then critically examined mainly to come out with an improved method, which increases the productivity. This necessitates the need for a precise recording technique for effective method study.

The common way of recording any information is to write it down. But writing down all the details of a complicated process in an industrial situation is not an easy task. In order to avoid these difficulties, certain graphical symbols of representations are adopted.

The advantages of such a form of recording are as listed below.

- It helps in presenting the necessary information in a precise and clear manner and facilitates further analysis.
- It is easily understandable and can be clearly visualized.

- Often presentation of the existing method or procedure, in a graphic form itself pinpoints obvious improvements.

Process Charts

The nature and order of the activities involved in a process are recorded using charts. A process chart is a visual representation of the steps that make up the work technique or procedure, with the various steps being represented by appropriate symbols. The usage of these symbols, which are labelled so as to be easily visible and to reflect conventional activities in a short hand form, simplifies the creation and comprehension of process charts. All activities can be broken down into five basic types of events and each is represented by a symbol.

The symbols that are used in the process charts are as given below.

i.   Operation
ii.   Inspection
iii. Transport
iv.   Delay
v.   Storage

The symbols that are used in the process charts are explained below.

Operation

When the physical or chemical properties of an object or material change, an operation takes place, which is symbolized by a circle. In process flow charts, the operation is denoted by the symbol that is displayed below.

Assembling and dis-assembling, preparing for an activity, moving semifinished job to output section of current workstation, etc. form examples of operation. In an office environment, writing a letter, preparing cover to post, taking files to another section form examples of operation.

Inspection

An inspection occurs when an object is checked for either quantity or quality. It is represented by a square symbol as shown below.

Some of the examples of the inspection are listed below.

- ➢ Checking the quantity of the components produced at a machine by counting.
- ➢ Verifying dimensional tolerances of a work piece.
- ➢ Visual inspection for surface quality of the components that are produced.
- ➢ Reading a letter that is received and taking action accordingly in an office.

Transport

A transport occurs whenever there is any movement either by the material or the man. The symbol of the transport activity is shown below.

Some of the examples of the transport activity are listed below.

- ➢ Movement of material on a trolley
- ➢ Man walking from a machine to machine
- ➢ Movement of an inspector from one inspection machine to another inspection machine.

Delay

A delay occurs when the next operation of the job that is being processed is not possible immediately. The symbol of the delay is as given below.

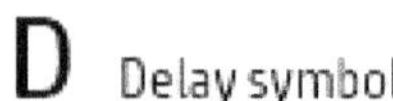

Some of the examples of the delay activity are as given below.

- ➢ Material waiting near a machine for an operation
- ➢ Operator waiting for a tool near the tool crib
- ➢ Operator waiting for the semifinished component from his preceding machine in a production line

Storage

A storage occurs when a semi-finished job is kept in a temporary storage area safely till it is moved to the work place. The symbol used to this activity is shown below. It is an inverted triangle.

Some examples of the storage symbol are as given below.

➢ Materials in store
➢ A letter in a file
➢ A subassembly waiting for the arrival of another subassembly to assemble the main product.

5.2.3.1 Flow Process Chart

The flow process chart that is used in industries is a graphical notation using suitable symbols to represent process steps of the job that is produced. This includes all the symbols, viz. operation, transport, inspection, delay and storage, which are associated with a job when it is manufactured. In this exercise, many charts are created, compared and the optimal way is then determined while keeping in mind the principles of motion economy.

Steps of Constructing Flow Process Chart

The steps of constructing the flow process chart are presented below.
i. Select the job/ component to be studied.
ii. Perform careful study of the complete operation of the job for few cycles.
iii. Record the activities of one hand (left hand and then right hand) at a time with corresponding symbols.
iv. The starting point of recording should be the beginning operation of the operation cycle associated with the job.
v. Enough care should be taken to include all the activities of the job in the chart.
vi. Care should be taken that no activity is left while recording, as it will affect the method study badly.

A two-handed process flow chart for nut and bolt assembly is shown in Fig.5.1.

5.2.3.2 Multiple Activity Charts

The process charts employing a time scale are called multiple activity charts. It typically enters the picture when a work study analyst needs to track one subject's actions in relation to another on a single chart. Worker, machine, or equipment are all potential subjects. Below is a list of the several varieties of the multiple activity chart.

- ➢ Man-Machine Activity Chart-when one operator is working on one machine.
- ➢ Multi-man Activity Chart-when a group of workers are working on a machine.
- ➢ Man- Multi machine activity chart- when a single operator is working on a number of machines.
- ➢ Multi man- Machine chart- a group of operators working on a common central machine.

Assembly of Nut and Bolt			
Left Hand	Symbol		Right Hand
	Left Hand	Right Hand	
Pickup bolt	◯	D	Idle
Hold	▽	◯	Pickup Nut
Hold	▽	⇨	To left Hand
Hold	▽	◯	Screw Up Nut Over Bolt

Fig.5.1 Two Handed Process Chart

This kind of chart is typically used to organize maintenance and similar tasks so that the amount of time expensive equipment is out of working is kept to a minimum. It goes without saying that easier methods exist for recording complex processes. It has uses in both group project planning and construction work.

5.2.4 Man-Machine Chart

The man-machine chart, or Simo chart are used in industrial planning to graphically define resource activity during repetitive operations. In Fig.5.2, a prototype man-machine diagram is presented. In this chart, each subject is given its own bar or column. These subjects are compared to a common chronological scale. By highlighting the corresponding bars or columns, activities of the worker and the machines are recorded. The time values of each action are provided from earlier time studies. Now, the activities are plotted in sequence against the common time scale. Once, the chart is constructed, the investigator has to analyze the portions of the idle times and work towards minimizing such idle time portions through improved method.

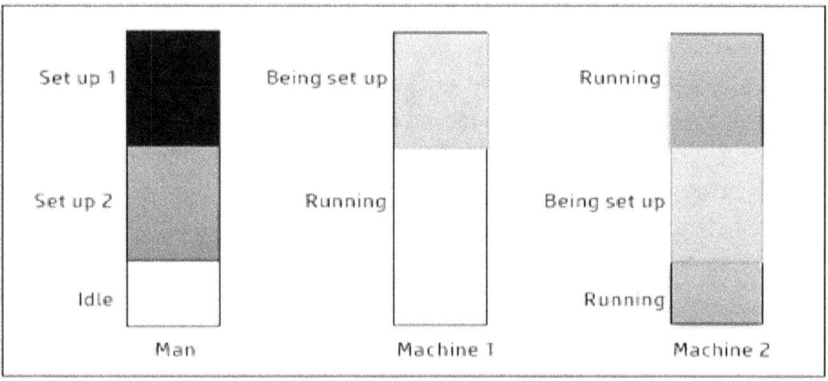

Fig 5.2 Man-machine Chart for one worker and two machines

5.2.5 SIMO Chart

Simultaneous cycle chart is referred to as SIMO. One of Gilbert's micro motion studies, it visually depicts the distinct steps taken by each relevant limb of the operator being studied. It is a left- hand and right-hand operating chart that is incredibly thorough. This chart simultaneously records the various therbligs carried by various bodily parts of one additional operator. The SIMO chart for the left hand and right -hand analysis sheet provides information on the level of involvement of both hands. A SIMO chart can be used to scale the times for each Therblig that are listed on the analysis sheet. The SIMO chart may be created separately or using data from the website, depending on the situation.

The SIMO chart is critically examined in order to grasp a picture of complete cycle in total details and assists in working out better combination of the desired motions.

The guidelines for constructing the SIMO chart are presented below.

i.   The nonproductive Therbligs such as search, select position and plan, etc. are to be re-examined with a view to eliminate these basic elements as much as possible.
ii. The investigator should focus towards productive Therbligs like transport loaded, disassemble, assemble and use, etc., in order to re-sequence for reducing the total cycle time and the extent of fatigue on the operators.
iii. The laws of motion economy should be used to improve the existing technique used by the operator for an operation.

5.2.6 String Diagram

String diagram is an important method used in method study. It can be characterized as a scale model on which a string is used to track the paths or motions of people and materials over the course of a predetermined series of events. The equipment and furniture in work areas should be positioned in the work place such that the work becomes easier. As a result, future work necessitates far more movement than is necessary. One of the issues is that it might be challenging to see what movements would be required while planning a workplace. The string diagram is also treated as flow diagram, which depicts the movements of operators and materials in the shop floor. Since, the string diagram uses the distance between each pair of locations where the operations are carried out, it is better to draw a scaled model. A careful examination of the existing string diagram will help the investigator to alter the routes of performing different operations in the shop floor. A sample string diagram is shown in Fig.5.3.

Steps of Constructing String Diagram

The steps of constructing the string diagram are listed below.

1. Examine and note relevant data regarding the transfer of different resources.
2. Sketch a scale schematic of the shop space, noting equipment, workbenches, st ores, and other elements.
3. On a paper board, mark the locations of the workstations, from where materials, and men move away or travels towards them using pins.
4. Remove the string to measure their lengths which approximately gives distances traveled by a worker or a machine or the material.
5. Using the data collected in the Step 4, rearrange the workstations to minimize the movements of materials and men.

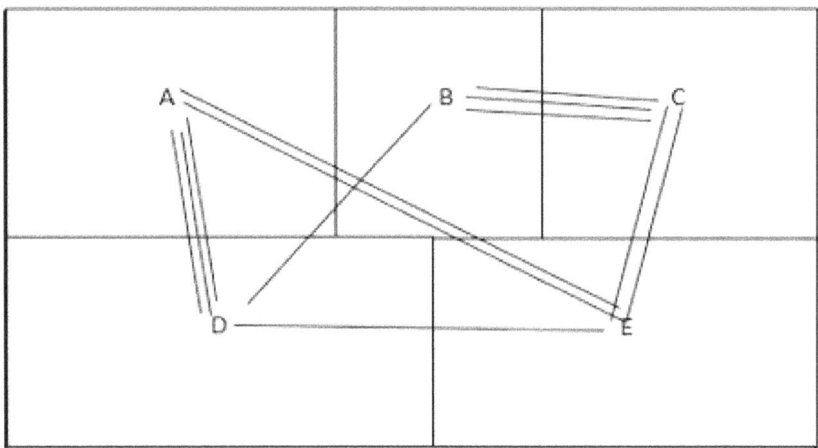

Fig.5.3 String Diagram

5.2.7   Cycle Graph

These methods, which were initially created by Gilbert are used to examine the motion pathways taken by an operator. A tiny electic bulb is fatened to the finger, hand, or other body part whose motion is being recorded in order to create a cycle graph. The path of a light bulb as it moves across space for an entire cycle is captured using still photography. A closed loop of a white cointinuous line with the working area in the background serves as a permanent record of the motion pattern used in the picture that is produced after the film has been developed. This graph will not indiacte direction or speed of the movement of the body part (tiny electric bulb).

5.2.8 Chrono-cycle Graph

The chrono cycle graph is an improved version of the cycle graph, which reflects the direction and speed of the body movement to which a light source is attached. In this graph, the complete cycle is recorded using micromotion study equipment, which attaches a light source to the moving body part to trace its path which appears as a series of pear-shaped dots, whose pointed ends indicates the direction of movement and the spacing between the dots gives speed of movement. The time is obtained by interrupting the light circuits with a controlled frequency which produces dots on the film.

5.2.9 Principles of Motion Economy

The principles of motion economy are a collection of guidelines and recommendations to enhance manual labor in manufacturing and lessen worker fatigue and superfluous motions, which can reduce work-related trauma.

The principles of motion economy can be classified into four groups.

- ➢ Principles related to the use of human body,
- ➢ Principles related to the arrangement of the work place,
- ➢ Principles related to the design of tools and equipment.
- ➢ Principles related to time conservation.

5.2.9.1 Principles of Motion Economy Based on Use of Human Body

The principles of the motion economy based on human body are listed below.

- ➢ The two hands should begin motions at the same time.
- ➢ The two hands should not be idle at the same time except during rest periods.
- ➢ Motions of the arms should be made in opposite and symmetrical directions and should be made simultaneously, which means that they should begin at the same time, but in opposite directions, and end at the same time.
- ➢ Hand motions should be restricted to the lowest parts of the hand as listed below.
  - i. Finger motions
  - ii. Wrist motions
  - iii. Forearm motions
  - iv. Upper arm motions
  - v. Shoulder motions

5.2.9.2 Principles of Motion Economy Based on Arrangement of the Work Place

The principles of the motion economy based on the arrangement of the workplace are as listed below.

- ➢ There should be a definite and fixed place for all tools and materials.
- ➢ Tools, materials, and controls should be located closer to the operator and in front of that operator.
- ➢ Drop delivers are favored whenever possible.
- ➢ Materials and tools should be located to permit the best sequence of motions.
- ➢ Arrange the height of the workplace and chair for alternate sitting and standing as per necessity.
- ➢ Provision of a chair of the type and height which will permit good posture to the operator to improve the productivity of the operator.

5.2.9.3 Principles of Motion Economy Based on Design of Tools and Equipment

The principles of the motion economy based on the design of tools and equipment are as listed below.

- ➢ Combine tools whenever possible, which will reduce the cycle time of operation.
- ➢ Prepositioned tools and materials will reduce the time taken for a given operation.
- ➢ Where each finger performs some specific movement, the load should be distributed in accordance with the inherent capacities of the fingers
- ➢ Momentum should be used to help the worker for increased productivity.

5.2.9.4 Principles of Motion Economy Based on Time Conservation

The principles of the motion economy based on the time conversion are as listed below.

- ➢ Avoid encouraging temporary delay of work by a man or machine.
- ➢ Plan the machine cycle such that the machine is not run-in idle condition.
- ➢ Plan the work cycle such that more than one operation is carried out on the job simultaneously, wherever possible.
- ➢ The job content should be such that the number of motions involved in completing a job is minimized.

5.3 WORK MEASUREMENT

Work measurement is the use of methodologies to determine how long it takes the typical worker to complete a particular manufacturing operation at a specific level of performance. It is concerned with how long it takes to finish a task that is given to a certain job. Work measurement is the estimation of the standard time for an activity, or the time allotted for finishing a single task using the recommended technique. Standard time is the amount of time needed to complete a task by a typical experienced worker allowing for unforeseen delays.

The Work measurement assists in identifying workplace non-standardization, waste, and activities that don't add value.

A work has to be measured for the following aspects.
1. To identify and eliminate ineffective time.
2. To determine standard times of the operations for performance measurement.
3. To measure performance of the man machine system of the shop floor against realistic benchmarks.
4. To set operating goals and objectives aligned with the overall system of manufacturing.

The techniques of the work measurement are as listed below.

i. Time study
ii. Work sampling
iii. Predetermined motion time system

5.3.1   Time study

A work measurement technique called time study involves carefully timing a task with a timer, adjusting for any observed deviation from normal effort or pace, and allowing enough time for things like unavoidable delays from equipment, breaks to recover from fatigue, and individual needs.

5.3.1.1 Steps of Time Study

The steps of the time study are as given below.

i.   Obtain and record all information pertaining to the job that is being considered.
ii.   Divide the job into meaningful smaller work elements and record them on an observation sheet.
iii.   Decide the number of cycles to be measured.
iv.   Observe stop watch times of the work elements and record them.
v.   Fine the average of the observed times
vi.   Judge the performance rating of the operator, who performs the operation elements.
vii.   Find the normal time using the performance rating.

$$Normal\ Time = Average\ of\ Observed\ Times$$
$$\times\ Performance\ Rating\ in\ Percentage$$

viii. Decide the allowances for delays, personal delays, fatigue delays and delays due to working conditions, etc.
ix.   Find the standard time from the normal time using the assumed allowance percentage. The formula to find the standard time is given

below.

$$\text{Standrad Time} = \text{Normal Time} \times \frac{1}{(1 - \text{Allowance percentage})}$$

$$= \frac{\text{Normal Time}}{(1 - \text{Allowance Percentage})}$$

5.3.1.2 Selection of job for Time Study

The selection of a job for the time study exercise is done if the following are true.
- No time study has been carried out on the job.
- No method change has been carried out recently.
- The job has tight time standard.

5.3.1.3 Selection of Worker for Time Study

The different considerations while selecting a worker for the time study exercise are as listed below.

- A key element in the study's success is the choice of workers for the time study. There isn't an option if there is only one person working, which is typically the case. However, the time study man may time one or more of the workers if more than one person is carrying out the same task.
- It is vital to choose a suitable worker for the study if all the workers use the same way to complete the task but do so at varying rates. The employee on whom the time study should be conducted must possess the appropriate skills.
- The employee needs to have adequate on-the-job experience using the prescribed procedure.
- The employee should work at a pace that is considered to be "typical" for workers.
- The employee should have a temperament that is appropriate for the study.
- The employee should be aware of the goal of the time study.

5.3.1.4 Time Study Equipment

The time study equipment that are needed to conduct the time study are as given below.
    i. Timing device
    ii. Time study observation sheet
    iii. Time study observation board
    iv. Other equipment

Timing Device

Although electronic timers are occasionally used, stop watches are the most common timing tool for time studies. The difference between the two is that an electronic timer can store a significant amount of time data in memory and measure time to the second/ third decimal of a second.

Time Study Observation Sheet

Time study observation sheet is a printed form containing slots for writing down the pertinent details regarding the operation being examined, including the name of the operation, the drawing number, the worker's name, the name of the time study person, and the date and location of the study. For writing a thorough description of the process, recorded time or stopwatch readings for each process operation, performance rating(s) of the operator, and computation, spaces are provided on the form.

Example 5.1

The time study engineer of a firm wants to find the standard time of a work element. He observed five cycles of the operation of the work element and the average observed time is 40 seconds. The performance rating of the operator who performed the operation is 110%. The total allowance percentage is 15%. Find the standard time of the work element.

Solution

Average observed time = 40 seconds
Performance rating of the operator = 110%
Total allowance = 15% =0.15

$$Normal\ Time = Average\ of\ Observed\ Times \times Performance\ Rating\ in\ Percentage$$
$$= 40 \times \frac{110}{100} = 44\ \text{seconds}$$

$$Standrad\ Time = \frac{Normal\ Time}{(1 - Allowance\ Percentage)} = \frac{44}{1 - 0.15} = 51.77\ seconds$$

5.3.2   Work Sampling

Work sampling is a statistical approach for calculating the percentage of time spent by employees engaged in several defined types of activity, such as assembling two parts, setting up a machine, etc. Work sampling is a method for gathering information on how equipment or people are used by making a large number of immediate observations at random periods. Establishing time requirements for both direct and indirect labor activities might greatly from work sampling. It is possible to provide a step-by-step description of the process for carrying out a work sampling study to determine the standard time of a job.

In work sampling, a job which has more than one operation is considered for study. All the operations of the job are performed by the same operator. The time study assistant will make a predetermined number of trips to the job spot and he/ she will note down the status of each operation in terms of whether that operation is performed or not performed in that trip. So, at the end of the study period, the frequency of performing each operation will be available. The percentage of working of an operation *i* is obtained using the formula as stated below.

$$\text{Percentage of working of operation } i$$
$$= \frac{\text{Frequency of performance of the operation } i}{\text{Total number of times the patroling person visited the job site}} \times 100$$

The multiplication of the percentage working of the operation *i* with the total duration of the study gives the observed time of the operation *i*. The multiplication of the observed time of the operation *i* with its performance rating of the operator with respect to that operation gives its normal time. The multiplication of the normal time of the operation *i* with its allowance fraction gives its standard time. The sum of the standard times of all the operations of the job gives the standard time of that job.

5.3.2.1 Steps in Work Sampling

The steps of work sampling are listed below.

1.   Define the operations of the job for which its standard time to be calculated.

2.   Define the components of the job.

    The main job is to be broken down into meaningful number of components/ operations. Also, make sure that idle time, waiting portion of the work, etc., are included in these tasks. Let the number of operations in the job that is studied be *n*.

3.   Plan the study
    Design the forms that will be used to record observations, figure out how many observations will be needed, decide how many days or shifts will be included in the study, planning the observations, and finally deciding how many observers will be required are included in this process.

4.   Decide which observer will conduct the work sampling.

5.   Inform the conduct of the study to concerned workers.

6.   Make random visits to plant and note any operations such as whether the operator is working, not working, machine is working or not working, etc. along with reasons for them if not working.

7.   Determine the production volume of the job during the duration of the work sampling.

8.   Compute the normal time of the operation i based on the data collected in Step 6 using the following formula.

$Normal\ time\ of\ the\ operation\ i =$

$$\frac{Duration\ of\ work\ sampling \times Percentage\ working_i \times Perfoemance\ rating_i}{Prudction\ volume\ of\ the\ job\ during\ the\ duration\ of\ work\ sampling},$$

$$i = 1, 2, 3, \ldots, n$$

Where,

$Percentage\ of\ working$

$$= \frac{Frequency\ of\ performance\ of\ the\ operation}{Total\ number\ of\ times\ the\ patroling\ person\ visited\ the\ job\ site} \times 100$$

9. Compute the standard time of the operation i using the following formula.

$$Standtad\ time\ of\ operation\ i = \frac{Normal\ time\ of\ operation\ i}{(1 - alloeance\ fraction)}, i = 1, 2, 3, \ldots, n$$

Where, allowance fraction is the decimal form of the allowance percentage (e.g. 10% = 0.1)

10. Find the standard time of the job using following formula.

$$Standard\ time\ of\ the\ job = \sum_{i=1}^{n} Standrad\ time\ of\ operation\ i$$

Where, *n* is the number of operations in the job that is being studied

Example 5.2

A time study analyst aims to find the standard time of a job which has three operations performed by the same operator. The study was conducted for one shift of 8 hours duration. The data of the work sampling study are shown in Table 5.1. The operator had produced 200 units in that shift. The allowance percentage is 10%. Find the standard time of the job.

Table 5.1 Summary of Data

Work element number	Frequency of performance	Performance rating
1	40	95%
2	85	120%
3	75	110%

Solution

The duration of the study = one shift = 480 minutes
No. of acceptable units produced/day = 200
Allowance = 10%
The summary of the calculations of the standard times of the operations of the job can be seen in Table 5.2.

Table 5.2 Summary of Calculations of Standard Times of Operations of Job

Work element	Frequency in one shift	Percentage working $\left(\dfrac{Frequency\ of\ working}{Total\ no.\ of\ trips}\right)$	Performance rating	Normal time (Minutes)	Standard time (Minutes)
1	40	20%	95%	(480*0.2*0.95)/200 = 0.456	0.506667
2	85	42.5%	120%	9480*0.425*1.2)/200=1.224	1.36
3	75	37.5%	110%	(480*0.375*1.1)/200=0.99	1.1
	$\Sigma = 200$			Standard time	2.966667

The standard time of the job with three operations = 2.988887 minutes = 2.99 min

5.3.2.2 Advantages and Disadvantages of Work Sampling in Comparison with Time Study

The advantages of the work sampling method are as given below.

- No stopwatch or other timekeeping equipment is required for work sampling study.
- Observations may be made over a few days or few weeks.

The following is a list of the drawbacks of the work sampling approach.

- Work sampling is not cost-effective for the investigation of one person, one activity, or one machine.
- Additionally, work sampling research may not be cost effective when looking at operators or equipment spread over large areas.
- The work sampling research does not offer fundamental time information about individual work elements.

Performance Rating in Work Sampling

The time study engineer closely monitors the operator's performance throughout the time study. This performance satisfies the exact requirements of what is normal or acceptable. As essential element in the work measurement process is determining the performance rating. It is fully based on the work-study engineer's knowledge, skills and judgment. The process by which the time study engineer compares the performance of the operator(s) under observation to the normal performance and establishes a factor known as the rating factor is known as performance rating.

5.3.3 Predetermined Motion Time System

A predefined motion time system (PMTS) is a process that examines every manual task in terms of the fundamental or most basic movements needed to complete it. Each of these actions is given a predetermined standard time value, and the timings for the separate motions are then combined to determine the overall amount of time required to complete the activity.

The applications of PMTS are listed below.

- ➢ Determination of time standards of jobs.
- ➢ This can be used to compare the times of alternative proposed methods and select the economical method.
- ➢ This can be used to estimate the manpower requirement, equipment, work space before constructing the plant.
- ➢ This will help to design tentative layouts even before starting the production, which can be altered once the production is started by taking real data from the shop floor.
- ➢ This will help to verify the conventional time study results.

5.3.3.1 Advantages and Limitations of Using PMT Systems

The advantages of PMTS are listed below.

- Using PMT compels the analyst to thoroughly research the methodology.
- This can occasionally help to refine the process even more.
- The PMTS times can be used to establish fundamental standard data for establishing time standards for tasks carried out on different types of machinery and equipment.
- The adoption of PMT does away with the necessity for problematic and divisive performance ratings.
- The PMT system yields basic times that are comparatively more reliable.

The limitations of the PMTS are as given below.

- The only manual aspects of the job are covered by its application, and skilled individuals are required.
- Even if the PMT system does away with ratings, some judgement must still be used at certain levels.

5.3.3.2 Application of Predetermined Motion Time Standards

Some of the key applications of PMTS in industries are as presented below.

- ➢ Determination of job time standards.
- ➢ Comparing the times for alternative proposed methods so as to find the economics of the proposals prior to production run.
- ➢ Estimation of manpower, equipment and space requirements prior to setting up the facilities and start of production.
- ➢ Developing tentative work layouts for assembly lines prior to their working in order

to minimize the amount of subsequent re-arrangement and re-balancing.
➤ Checking direct time study results.

REVIEW QUESTIONS

1. Define method study and explains objectives.
2. Explain the steps of the method study.
3. List and explain the process chart symbols.
4. What is flow process chart? Explain the steps of constructing it.
5. What are the types of multiple activity charts? Briefly explain them.
6. What is man-machine chart? Illustrate it with an example.
7. What is SIMO chart? Illustrate it with an example.
8. What is string diagram? Illustrate it with an example.
9. Explain the following.
   a. Cycle graph
   b. Chrono cycle graph
10. Explain the principles of motion economy.
11. What are techniques of work measurement? Explain them in brief.
12. Define time study and explain its steps.
13. Explain the following.
    a) Time study equipment
    b) Time study observation sheet
14. The time study engineer of a firm wants to find the standard time of a work element. He observed five cycles of the operation of the work element and the average observed time is 50 seconds. The performance rating of the operator who performed the operation is 130%. The total allowance percentage is 12%. Find the standard time of the work element.
15. Define work sampling and explain its steps.
16. The time study analyst aims to find the standard time of a job which has four operations performed by the same operator. The study was conducted for one shift of 8 hours duration. The data of the work sampling study are shown in the following table. The operator had produced 250 units in that shift. The allowance percentage is 12%. Find the standard time of the job.

Summary of Data

Work element number	Frequency of performance	Performance rating
1	40	90%
2	90	130%
3	70	115%
4	50	120%

17. What is predetermined motion time system? Explain its applications in industries.
18. Discuss the advantages and limitations of PMTS.
19. Discuss the application of Predetermined Motion Time Standards

CHAPTER 6 PRODUCTION PLANNING AND CONTROL

6.1 INTRODUCTION

Production planning is the organization of the manufacturing and production processes within a business or sector. In order to service clients, it makes use of the resource allocation of activities of employees, materials and production capacity. Production planning is a strategy for future production in which the necessary facilities are identified and set up. Periodically, for a predetermined amount of time known as the planning horizon, a production plan is made.

The following operations are included in production planning and control:

- Determining the production load and product mix needed to meet consumer demands.
- Aligning the necessary level of production with the available resources.
- Planning and selecting the specific task that will begin in the production plant.
- Configuring and sending manufacturing orders to production facilities.

The marketing department and sales department must collaborate closely with the production planner or production planning department to produce production plans. They can prepare a list of customer orders or sales projections. The precise evaluation of the productive capacity of the available resources is a crucial component of production planning, but it is also one of the trickiest things to master. Planning for production should always consider the availability of raw materials, resources, and information about anticipated demand. The production planning process is broken down into the following steps, which are depicted in Fig. 6.1.

- Execute
- Check results
- Replan and reinvestigate changes

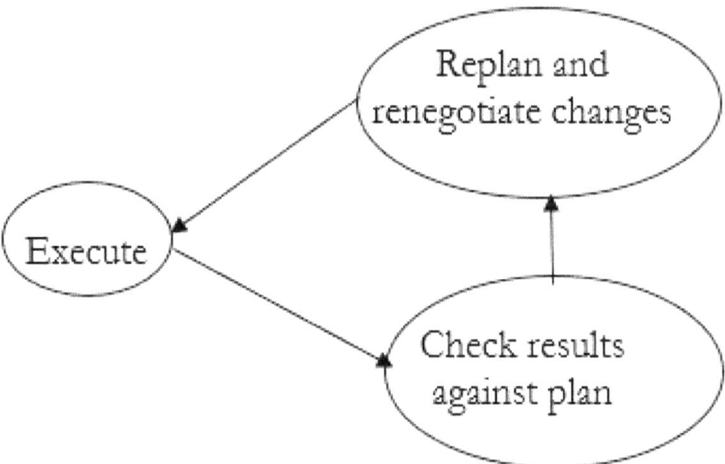

Fig.6.1 Macro steps of production planning and Control

6.2 Functions of Production Planning and Control

The function of the production planning and control are as listed below.

i.   Forecasting
ii.   Materials planning
iii.   Process selection and planning
iv.   Facility location
v.   Estimating quantity and cost of production
vi.   Line planning
vii.   Scheduling
viii.   Loading production line
ix.   Follow up and execution

6..2.1 Forecasting

Making predictions about the future based on data from the past and present and trend analysis is the process of forecasting. An everyday example would be to estimate a variable of interest at a certain future time. The two main components of forecasting and prediction are risk and uncertainty. It is usually regarded as best practice to describe the level of uncertainty associated with projections. In any event, for the forecast to be as precise as possible, the data must be current. Fig. 6.2 depicts a sample graph illustrating the projection of the two various products through time.

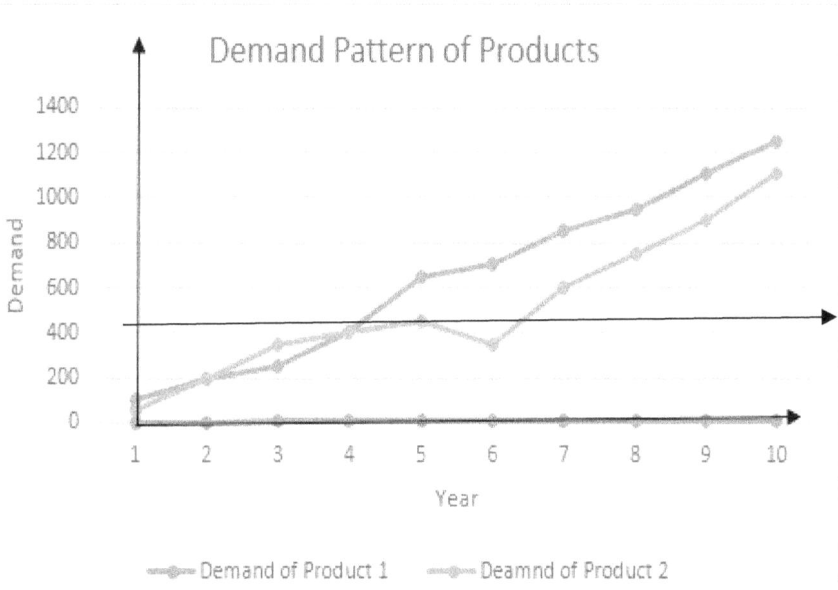

Fig.6.2 Forecasting graph

6.2.1.1 Categories of Forecasting Methods

The categories of forecasting methods are as listed below.
- ➢ Quantitative forecasting
- ➢ Qualitative forecasting

Quantitative Forecasting

In order to predict future data as a function of historical data, quantitative forecasting models are used. When prior numerical data is accessible and it is fair to believe that some of the patterns in the data will likely persist into the future, they are appropriate for use.

Qualitative Forecasting

Techniques for qualitative forecasting are based on the judgement and opinion of experts and consumers, and are appropriate when historical data is not accessible. They are typically used while making long- or intermediate-range choices. Market research, the Delphi method, and informed opinion and judgement are a few examples of qualitative forecasting techniques.

6.2.1.2 Forecasting Methods

There are several methods of forecasting, which are as listed below.
- i. Moving average method

ii.   Exponential shooting method

iii.   Regression method

6.2.1.2.1   Moving Average Method

Mean of data from multiple successive periods of time series, or evenly spaced observations is referred to as moving average because it is continuously recomputed as new data become available. As it advances, the earliest value is removed and the most recent value is added. For instance, by averaging the sales from January to March, one can get the moving average of three-month sales.

A moving average is also known as a rolling average, which is computed in statistics to examine data points by averaging a number of different subsets of the entire data set. Another name for it is a moving mean. The first component of the moving average is created by averaging the initial subset of a sequence of values with a fixed subset size.

Example 6.1

Auto sales of a popular brand in thousands are shown in Table 6.1. Develop a 3-week moving average for the week 6, which acts as the forecast for the week 7.

Table 6.1 Auto Sales Data

Week	Auto sales
1	8
2	10
3	9
4	11
5	10
6	12
7	?

Solution

The formula for the moving average of the previous n periods is as given below.

$$Moving\ average\ of\ previous\ n\ periods\ accounted\ at\ the\ end\ of\ period\ n$$

$$= \frac{Sum\ of\ the\ demands\ of\ pervious\ n\ periods}{n}$$

If the number of weeks for the moving average is assumed to be 3, then the calculations of the three-year moving averages (MA_t, t = 3, 4, 5) are shown in the third column of the Table 6.2. The moving average of the week t is treated as the forecast for the week t+1 as shown in the last column of the Table 6.2. The moving average of the week 6 is 11 units. Hence, the forecast of the week 7 is 11 units.

Table 6.2 Auto Sales Data with Three Week Moving Averages

Week (t)	Auto sales (D_t)	Moving average (MA_t)	Forecast (F_t)
1	8	-	-
2	10	-	-
3	9	$\dfrac{8 + 10 + 9}{3} = 9$	-
4	11	$\dfrac{10 + 9 + 11}{3} = 10$	9
5	10	$\dfrac{9 + 11 + 10}{3} = 10$	10
6	12	$\dfrac{11 + 10 + 12}{3} = 11.$	10
7	?		11

6.2.1.2.2 Exponential Smoothing Method

By ignoring fluctuations that are not relevant to the current goal, statistical methods can identify important changes in data. In exponential smoothing, recent data is given more weight than older data, but both types of data are preferred. To accurately predict demand using this method, one can use two or more smoothing parameters (smoothening parameters are alpha and beta).

The following formula uses the exponential smoothing approach to calculate the forecast for period t.

$$F_t = F_{t-1} + \alpha(D_{t-1} - F_{t-1})$$

Where, F_t is the exponential smoothed forecast for the period t
F_{t-1} is the exponential smoothed forecast for the period t-1
D_{t-1} is the demand of the period t-1
α is the smoothing constant, whose value is from 0.1 to 0.3.

Example 6.2

The demand of an item fluctuates daily. The demand values of the past five days are shown in Table 6.3. Find the forecast of the Day 2, Day 3, Day 4 and day 5 by assuming a smoothing constant of 0.3 and the forecast of the Day 1 (F_1) as 14000 units.

Table 6.3 Daily Demand of Item

Day	1	2	3	4
Demand (Units)	15000	16000	18000	20000

Solution

The data of the given example are reproduced in Table 6.4.

Table 6.4 Daily Demand Values of Item

Day	1	2	3	4
Demand	15000	16000	18000	20000

The formula to find the forecast of the day t is given below.

$$F_t = F_{t-1} + \alpha(D_{t-1} - F_{t-1})$$

Where, F_t is the exponential smoothed forecast for the period t
F_{t-1} is the exponential smoothed forecast for the period t-1
D_{t-1} is the demand of the period t-1
α is the smoothing constant, whose value is from 0.1 to 0.3.

The forecasts for Day 2, Day 3, Day 4 and Day 5 are computed as shown below.

$$F_2 = F_1 + \alpha(D_1 - F_1) = 14000 + 0.3 \times (15000 - 14000) = 14300 \text{ units}$$
$$F_3 = F_2 + \alpha(D_2 - F_2) = 14300 + 0.3 \times (16000 - 14300) = 14810 \text{ units}$$
$$F_4 = F_3 + \alpha(D_3 - F_3) = 14810 + 0.3 \times (18000 - 14810) = 15767 \text{ units}$$
$$F_5 = F_4 + \alpha(D_4 - F_4) = 15767 + 0.3 \times (20000 - 15767) = 17036.9 \text{ units}$$

6.2.1.2.3 Regression Method

Regression analysis is a statistical method for determining the relationships between variables in statistical modelling. When the emphasis is on the link between a dependent variable and one or more independent variables, it encompasses numerous approaches for modelling and evaluating multiple variables. The format of the data generation process and how it connects to the regression methodology being utilized determine how well regression analysis approaches perform in practice.

The independent and dependent variables' causal relationships can be inferred using regression analysis. However, caution is advised because this could result in illusions or false associations. The performance of regression analysis methods in practice depends on the shape of the data that fits into a distribution, and how it relates to the regression methodology being employed. Since the exact nature of the method used to generate the data is typically unknown, regression analysis frequently relies to some level on making assumptions about it.

The model of the simple linear regression is given below.

$Y = a + bX$

where,

X is the independent variable
Y is the dependent variable
a is the intercept of the regression model
b is the slope of the regression model

The graph of this model is as given in Fig.6.3.

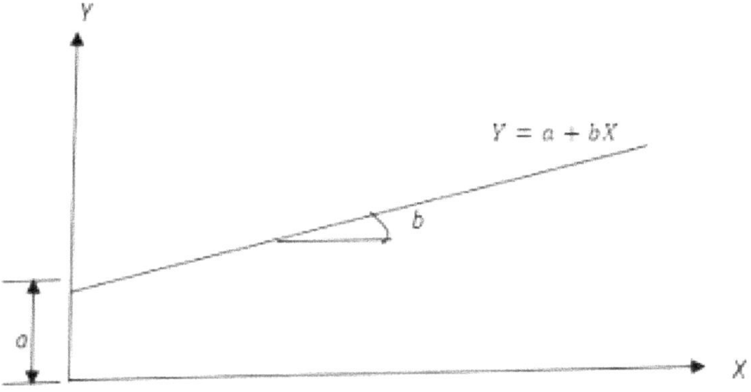

Fig.6.3 Graph of regression model

The formulas to compute the coefficients of the model are given below.

$$b = \frac{\sum XY - n\bar{X}\bar{Y}}{\sum X^2 - n\bar{X}^2}$$

$$a = \bar{Y} - b\bar{X}$$

Example 6.3

The demand values in units of a product during the past 7 years are summarized in Table 6. 5. Fit a linear regression model and estimate the demand of the product for the year 8.

Table 6.5 Summary of Data of Demand

Year	Demand in units
1	2000
2	2200
3	2700
4	2600
5	3000
6	3500
7	3400

Solution

The data of this problem with additional details to compute the coefficients of the regression model are shown in Table 6.6.

The regression model is as given below

$$Y = a + b\,X$$

where,

X is the independent variable to represent the time period 'Year'
Y is the dependent variable to represent the demand of the product
a is the intercept of the regression model
b is the slope of the regression model

The formulas to compute the coefficients of the model are given below.

$$b = \frac{\sum XY - n\bar{X}\bar{Y}}{\sum X^2 - n\bar{X}^2}$$

$$a = \bar{Y} - b\bar{X}$$

Table 6.6 Summary of Data of Demand with Calculations

	Year	Demand in units	X^2	XY
	1	200	1	200
	2	210	4	420
	3	270	9	810
	4	260	16	1040
	5	300	25	1500
	6	350	36	2100
	7	340	49	2380
Sum	28	1930	140	8450
Mean	4	275.714286		

$$b = \frac{\sum XY - n\bar{X}\bar{Y}}{\sum X^2 - n\bar{X}^2} = \frac{8450 - 7\times4\times275.714286}{140 - 7\times4^2} = 26.07143$$

$$a = \bar{Y} - b\bar{X} = 257.714286 \times 26.07143 \times 4 = 171.4286$$

The model is as given below.

$$Y = 171.4286 + 26.07143 \times X$$

The demand Y for the year 8 = $171.4286 + 26.07143 \times 8 = 380\ units$

6.2.2 MATERIALS PLANNING

Material planning is concerned with creating a material need sheet based on a buyer specification sheet and a sample product. The amount of material consumed and the expected cost of each material are computed.

6.2.3 Process Selection and Planning

The steps required to complete an order differ depending on the style. PPC department chooses processes for the orders based on the requirements of the order (client). Sometimes additional procedures are removed to reduce production costs.

6.2.4   Facility Location

The planner must determine which factory will be best suited for new orders in cases where a company has multiple factories (facilities) for production and factories are set up for specific products. When a manufacturer experiences a capacity issue, the planner must choose which facility will be chosen to fulfil the orders.

6.2.5   Estimating Quantity and Costs of Production

Planner calculate daily output (units) based on the nature of the work. Planners for production runs and human engagement also estimate production cost per item with the projected production amount.

6.2.6   Line planning

It is concerned with the preparation of a detailed line planning with daily production target for the production line.

6.2.7 Production Scheduling

Scheduling of time and tasks from order receipt to shipment for each order is called production scheduling. The list of work to be completed for the styles is included in the production schedule. The task planner indicates next to each task when it should be started and when the deadline is. The name of the job and the department in which it is produced are listed.

The process of allocating tasks to resources that can complete them is called scheduling. A scheduler may strive to achieve any number of objectives, such as lowering response time and increasing throughput in units of production.

The goal of scheduling in manufacturing is to save production time and costs by instructing a production facility on when to manufacture something, who should be involved and what tools to use. The goal of production scheduling is to increase operating efficiency and cut expenses on equipment requirements. Businesses utilize backward and forward scheduling to allocate resources for equipment and plants, plan for human resources, organize their manufacturing processes, and make material purchases. In order to determine the delivery date or the due date, tasks are scheduled in advance starting from the day resources become available. Backward scheduling involves determining the start data and or any necessary changes in capacity by planning the tasks from the due date. Figure6.4 depicts a sample schedule of purchase orders.

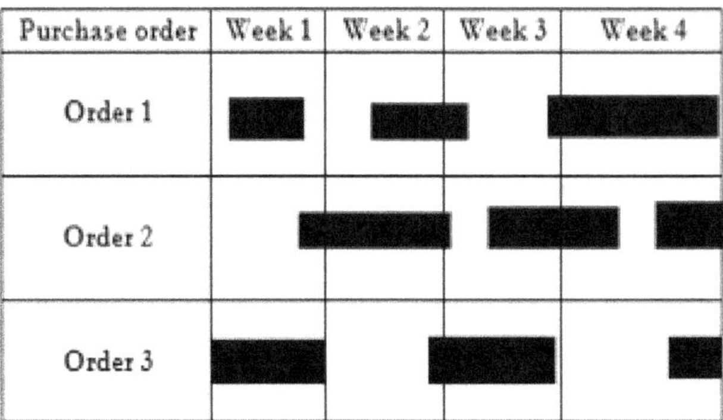

Fig.6.4 Sample schedule of purchase orders

6.3   MATERIALS MANAGEMENT

To make things on schedule for a certain consumer base, materials management aims to supply a continuous chain of production-related components. In order for materials to reach production stages on schedule, the materials department is in charge of releasing them to the supply base.

6.3.1 Goals of Materials Management

The following is a list of the materials management's goals.

- Keeping a steady supply of production materials is the fundamental difficulty that materials managers have.
- Incorrect bills of materials, erroneous cycle counts, unreported scrap, shipping, receiving, and production reporting errors are the main problems that all materials managers deal with.
- If the materials department is successful in lowering the cost of the goods it purchases, this will help to increase revenues while also lowering operational costs.
- Less money is locked up in inventories because stocks are kept in control in relation to sales.
- Maintaining a steady supply of materials is crucial to prevent production interruptions.
- Minimizing the costs of production increase when materials are not consistently available.
- The materials department is in charge of guaranteeing the quality of supplies from outside vendors. As a result, the most important objective in the selection of materials is quality.

6.3.2 Functions of Materials Management

The functions of the materials management are shown schematically in Fig.6. 5.

From the Fig.6.5, the list of the functions of the materials management is as given below.

- Ensuring demand-based procurement, which will reduce the inventory cost greatly.
- Issue of raw materials from the raw materials stores based on Just-In-Time principle, which will reduce in-process inventory in the shop floor.
- Design of proper inventory model for each item with appropriate safety stock and buffer stock.
- Synchronizing the stores operations with the shop floor production schedules for uninterrupted supply of raw materials to the shop floor.
- Continually monitoring stock on hand (SOH) with the reorder level (ROL) for each item to place orders if the SOH is less than or equal to the ROL of each item.

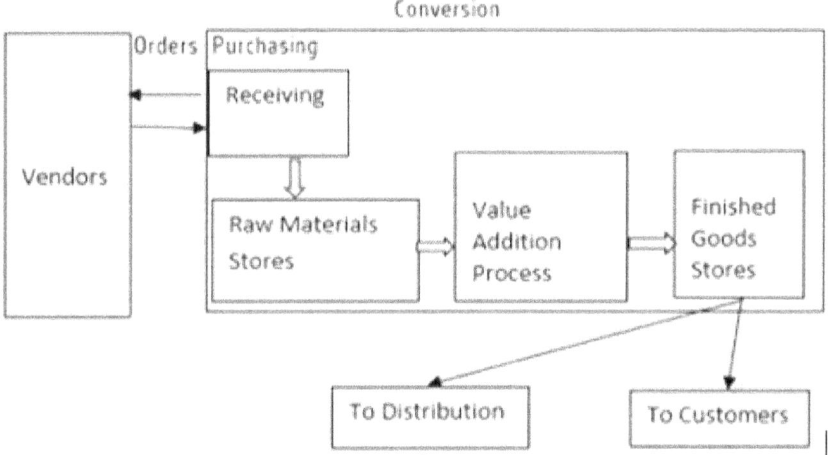

Fig.6.5 Functions of Materials Management

6.4   INVENTORY CONTROL

The definition of inventory control or stock control is 'the action of verifying a shop's stock. A method for organizing and locating commodities or things is an inventory control system, sometimes known as computerized inventory system.

Stock control system are now used in many stores. The items that a company keeps in stock, also known as inventory or stock, are those that are intended for eventual resale (or repair). The science of inventory management is largely concerned with describing the type and proportion of stocked products.

6.4.1   Need of Inventory

Inventory is a necessary for smooth operation of any business system. The reasons for maintaining inventory are listed below.

- Over inventory increases material cost in terms of additional inventory cost and under inventory leads to shortages of materials, which will result with lost order.

- The materials manager of every firm should maintain optimum inventory to minimize the cost of carrying the items in stock.
- The inventory system is augmented with raw material store attached to the firm to store and issue to the shop floor based on JIT principle to reduce inventory cost and at the same time to avoid stockouts.
- The inventory in the raw material stores helps to cope up with the fluctuating demand of the items that are produced in the firm. The inclusion of safety stock in the reorder level will avoid stockouts due to fluctuation in demand.
- Some of the items that are required to manufacture products are seasonal and/ or cyclical. Hence, a suitable inventory model is to be used.
- The lead times of the items that are purchased may vary, which introduces uncertainty. So, the inclusion of a proper buffer stock in the reorder level will reduce/avoid stockouts.
- The items are to be classified into high consumption value items, moderate consumption value items and low consumption value items. This will help to apply tight control, moderate control and less control, respectively on those items.

6.4.2   Functions of Inventory Control

The functions of the inventory control for smooth functioning of any organization are listed below.

- To meet the demand of customer without any delay.

- To smooth out the materials availability in the shop floor.

- To avoid stock out of components and subassemblies in the shop floor.

- To monitor the stock level of every component with reference to a preset reorder level to place order if the stock level is less than the reorder level.

- To know the quantity of material required for each component in each period of production.

- To have an estimate of the cost of each component/ subassembly that will be procured.

- Inventory management keeps track of a company's resources, such as labor, money and material goods that are used or sold.

- The objective of the company is to maintain certain operational requirements in terms of materials such that least amount is invested to operate inbound raw materials stores and outbound finished goods stores.

- It should focus in minimizing the wastages in the stores and production lines.

- The main purpose of inventory is to boost profitability by leveraging the production and marketing to maximize return on investment for the company

6.4.3 Types of Inventories

The different types of inventories are listed below.
- Raw materials inventory

- Work-in progress inventory
- Finished goods inventory
- Safety stock
- Buffer stock

Raw material inventory: The maker converts raw materials into components, subassemblies, or final goods as part of the manufacturing process. Components are often produced using raw materials. These parts are then included in the finished item or are added to a subassembly.

Work in progress: All the materials, parts (components), assemblies, and subassemblies that are now being processed or that are awaiting processing within the system are collectively referred to as "work-in-process" (WIP). All materials, from raw materials that have been released to start processing to materials that have been fully processed and are awaiting final inspection and acceptance before being incorporated into completed items, are typically included in this.

Finished goods inventory: A completed component that is prepared for a customer order is known as a finished good. As a result, finished goods inventory is the collection of finished goods. These products have undergone final inspection and passed, allowing for their transition from work-in-process to finished goods inventory. From this point, finished goods can be sold to retailers, wholesalers, distribution centers, or retained in anticipation of a client order. They can also be sold straight to their end user.

 Safety Stock and Buffer Stock: Inventory can serve as cushion against market fluctuations in supply and demand as well as unforeseen occurrences, while receiving raw materials from vendors.

Safety stock is the stock that will be maintained over and above the average demand during lead time, to cope up with the fluctuations in demand of a material/ component/ subassembly.

Buffer stock is the stock that will be maintained over and above the average demand during lead time, to cope up with the fluctuations in lead time of a material/ component/ subassembly.

A relative positioning of these inventory types is shown in Fig.6.6.

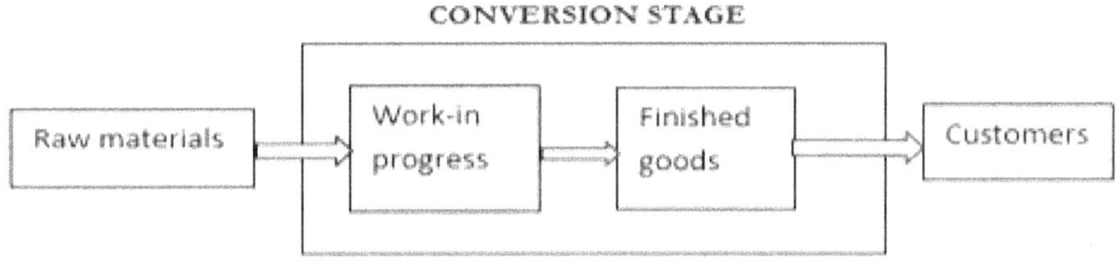

Fig.6.6 Relative positioning of the types of inventories

6.4.4   Inventory Models

Inventory theory is concerned with the control of product stock levels with the goal of meeting demand. Most models are created to handle the two basic decision-making problems that are stated below.

i.   The best time to place a replenishment order and the ideal order quantity.

ii.   Deciding on the optimal order size and frequency to ensure uninterrupted delivery of goods and services to customers, as well as designing production and inventory systems to cut costs.

The types of inventory model are as given below, which are presented in the following subsections.
a)   Economic order quantity (EOQ) model
b)   Fixed order quantity model
c)   Fixed order period model
d)   Single period model

6.4.4.1 Economic Order Quantity (EOQ) Model

The order quantity that minimizes the overall holding costs and ordering costs is known as the economic order quantity (EOQ). One of the first traditional production scheduling models is this one. EOQ only applies when a product's demand is steady throughout the year and every new order is fulfilled in full when inventory is zero. No matter how many units are ordered, there is a fixed cost for each order, which is known as ordering cost per order. Additionally, there is a charge for each unit kept in storage, known as the inventory carrying cost per unit per period, which is occasionally represented as a percentage of the item's purchase price. The determination of EOQ takes annual demand, ordering cost and carrying cost as inputs.

The total cost of the inventory system is the sum of the following costs.

i.   Purchase cost
ii.   Ordering cost
iii.   Inventory carrying cost

Total cost = Purchase cost + Ordering cost + Inventory carrying cost

Purchase cost is the unit price of the component/ subassembly that is purchased from a vendor. The ordering cost per order is the cost of ordering per order, which includes the cost of preparation of order copy, intimation of this copy to the vendor, monitoring the order status till the item against the order reaches the raw materials stores of the company. The inventory carrying cost per unit per period is the cost of holding an item in the store without use, which includes the cost of the storage space per unit per period, cost of administration per unit per period for that item to stock in the stores and the interest on the purchase cost per unit per period.

Figure 6.7 shows a graph that shows the trade-off among the ordering cost and the carrying cost. The total cost is the sum of these two costs, which is minimum for a particular order size of the item, which is known as Economic Order Quantity (EOQ).

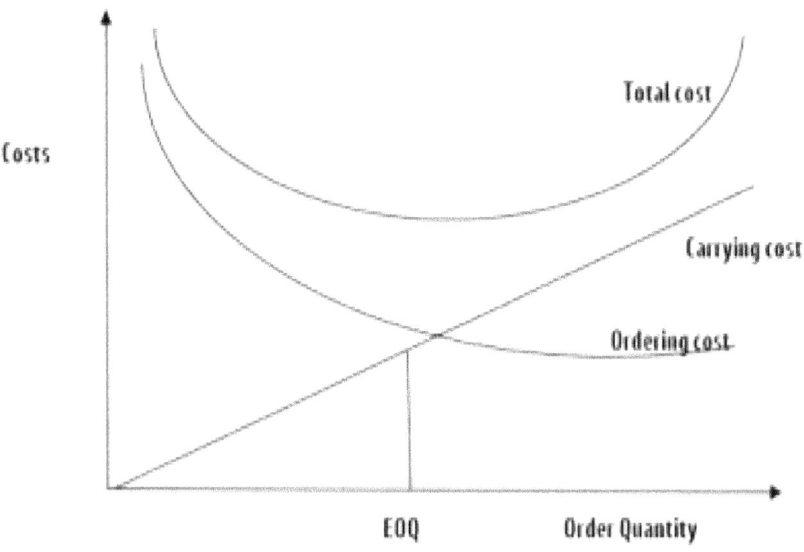

Fig.6.7 Graph showing EOQ and different costs

The formula to find the economic order quantity (EOQ) is given below.

$$EOQ = \sqrt{\frac{2C_o D}{C_c}}$$

Where, C_o is the cost per order

C_c is the carrying cost per unit per period

D is the demand per period

EOQ is the economic order quantity

$$Total\ cost\ of\ inventory\ (TC) = Ordering\ Cost + carrying\ Cost + Purcahse\ Cost$$
$$= \frac{D}{Q} \times C_o + \frac{Q}{2} \times C_c + p \times D$$

Where,

C_o is the cost per order

C_c is the carrying cost per unit per year

D is the demand per year

$Q^* = EOQ$, which is the economic order quantity

p is the price per unit

TC is the total cost of the inventory system

Example 6.4

A leading E-commerce company plans for the economic order size of a book, which costs 1,500 rupees per copy. The annual demand for this book is 10,000 copies. The ordering cost per order is Rs.5,000 and the carrying cost per unit per year is Rs.150. Determine the economic order quantity for this book.

Solution.

Annual demand of the book (D) = 10,000 copies
Ordering cost per order (C_o) = Rs.5,000
Carrying cost per book per year (C_c)= Rs.150.
Unit price (p) = Rs.1,500

$$EOQ = Q^* = \sqrt{\frac{2C_oD}{C_c}} = \sqrt{\frac{2\times5000\times10000}{150}} = 816.4966 = 817 \text{ copies}$$

$$Total\ cost\ of\ inventory\ system$$
$$= Ordering\ Cost + carrying\ Cost + Purcahse\ Cost$$

$$= \frac{D}{Q^*} \times C_o + \frac{Q'}{2} \times C_c + p \times D$$
$$= \frac{10000}{817} \times 5000 + \frac{817}{2} \times 150 + 1500 \times$$
$$10000 = Rs.\ 1,51,22,475$$

The implementation of this model with instantaneous replenishment is shown in Fig.6.8.

In the Fig.6.8, initially a stock of Q^* is maintained and it is consumed at uniform rate of D units per year. Then the stock level reaches zero after a time period of t^*. At that time, another lot of Q^* reaches instantaneously, which takes the stock level to Q^*. This cycle continues throughout the year.

The instantaneous supply of the lot against order can be modified into a realistic implementable model by including ROL. The reorder level (*ROL*) is given by the following formula.

$ROL = D_{LT} + SS + BB$

Where, D_{LT} is the demand during lead time
SS is the safety stock to cope up with fluctuations in demand during lead time

BS is the buffer stock to cope up with the fluctuations in in lead time during leading time.
ROL is the reorder level

In this model, the stock level will be continuously monitored and when the stock level touches the reorder level, immediately an order will be placed.

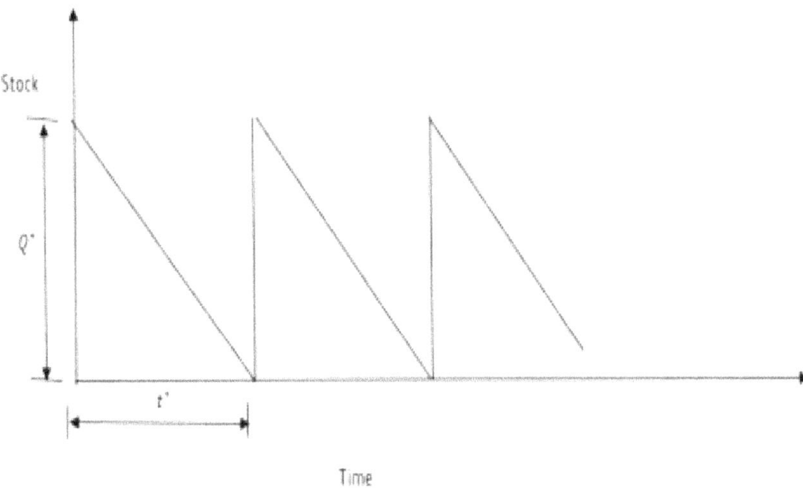

Fig.6.8 Implementation of purchase model of inventory with instantaneous replenishment

In a deterministic model in which the demand and lead time are constant, the ROL is given by the following formula.

$$ROL = D_{LT}$$

Where, D_{LT} is the demand during lead time

ROL is the reorder level

A deterministic model for the purchase model of inventory (Saw tool model) is shown in Fig.6.9.

Example 6.5

The demand of TV in a retail shop is 5000 units per year. The ordering cost per order is Rs.2000. The purchase price per unit of the TV is Rs.30,000. The lead time to deliver the items against the order is 2 weeks. The carrying cost per unit per year of the TV is 10% of its purchase price.

i.   Find the EOQ of the TV.

ii.   Find the ROL of the purchase model of inventory.

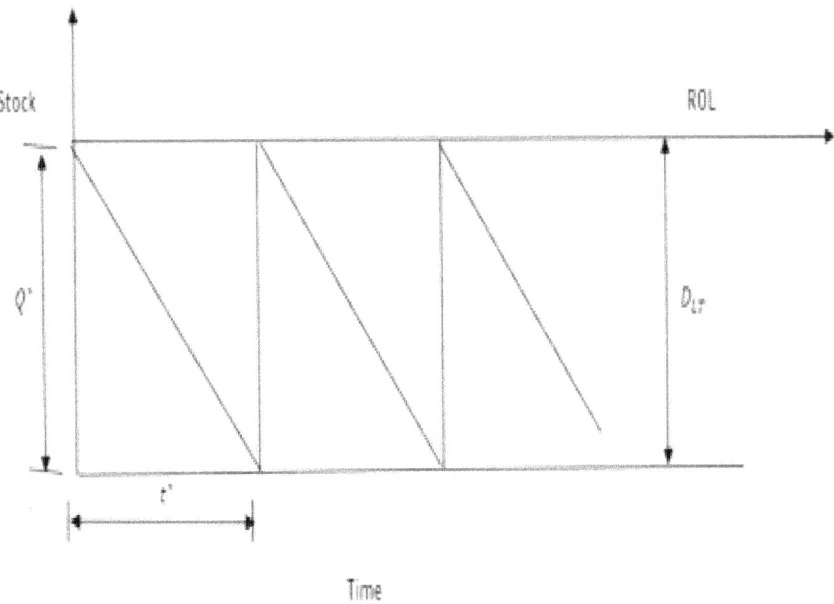

Fig.6.9 Implementation of purchase model of inventory with ROL

Solution.

Demand of TV (D) = 5000 units
Ordering cost per order (C_0) = Rs.2,000
Purchase cost per unit (p) = Rs.30,000
Carrying cost per unit per year (C_c)= 10% of purchase price per unit = 0.10×30,000 = Rs.3,000

Lead time (LT) = 2 weeks

i)   The economic order quantity is computed as under.

$$EOQ = Q^* = \sqrt{\frac{2C_0 D}{C_c}} = \sqrt{\frac{2 \times 2000 \times 5000}{3000}} = 81.65 = 82\ units$$

ii) $ROL = D_{LT} = \dfrac{D}{52} \times LT = \dfrac{5000}{52} \times 2 = 192.3\ Units$

6.4.4.2 Fixed Order Quantity Model (Q System)

While ordering an item, the order size may be the same or varying. If the order size (EOQ) is the same at all the times of ordering, then it is called as fixed order quantity model, which is known as Q system of inventory.

In this model, a reorder level (ROL) is maintained. If the stock on hand is less than or equal to the reorder level, then an order is placed. When the items against an order are received, the stock level is updated using the following formula.

Stock-On-Hand = Stock-On-Hand + Order Size (EOQ)

When an issue of the item is made to the shop floor, the stock level is updated using the following formula.

Stock-On-Hand = Stock-On-hand – Issue Quantity

The Fig.6.9 sets an example of the Q system of inventory.

6.4.4.3 Fixed Period Model (P System)

In this model, the time between consecutive orders is constant. This leads to varying order sizes while ordering the item. In this model, a maximum stock level is determined, which is the sum of the average demand during lead time, safety stock and buffer stock. The safety stock is the cushion for the variation in demand values during the lead time. The buffer stock is the cushion for the variation in lead time. The formulas for the maximum stock level and order size at the end of the given constant period are given below.

Maximum stock level = Average demand during lead time+ Safety stock + Buffer stock

Order quantity at the end of every fixed period = Maximum stock level – Stock on hand

6.4.4.4 Single Period Model

This model is applicable for perishable items. In this model, an optimal order size will be determined. When this is implemented, the unsold/ unused items will be disposed instead of carrying them to the next period. Hence, it is called as single period model.

6.4.5 Selective Inventory Model: ABC Analysis

The ABC categorization divides a variety of items in the stores into three categories. It has another name called selective inventory control.

The inventory is divided into three groups using the ABC analysis. A class items have very strict control and accurate records, B class items have less strict control but still good records, and C class have most basic control and the fewest records.

A graph showing the A, B and C class items on X axis and percentage consumption values on Y axis is shown in Fig.6.10.

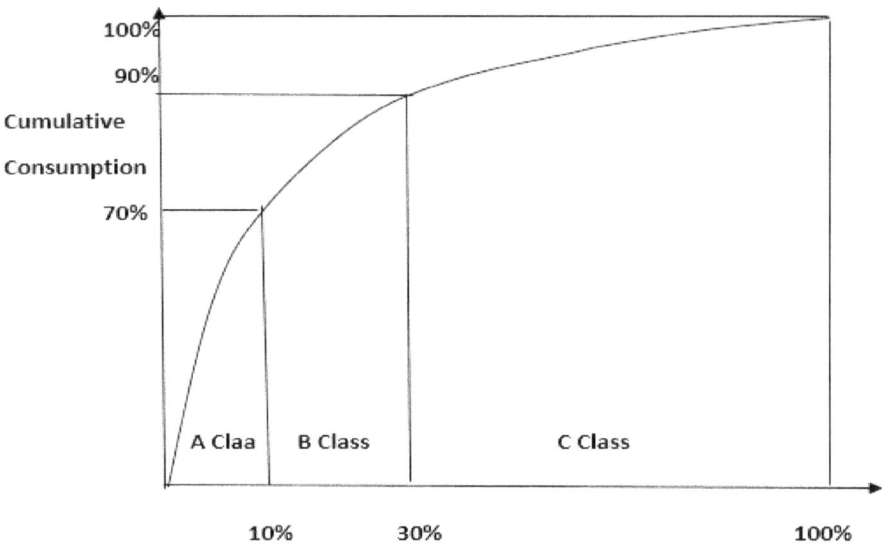

Fig.6.10 Graph of ABC Analysis

Ideal combinations the cumulative consumption value and the percentage number of items are shown below.

i.   A items: 10% of the items accounts for 70% of the annual consumption value of the items.

ii.   **'B'** items: 20% of the items accounts for 20% of the annual consumption value of the items.

iii.   **'C'** items: 70% of the items accounts for 10% of the annual consumption value of the items.

6.4.5.1 Steps of ABC Analysis

The steps of ABC analysis are presented below.

    i.   Gather data on unit price and volume of each part.

    ii.   Find the consumption value of each item by multiplying its volume by its unit price.

    iii.   Sort the items along with data in the decreasing order of the consumption values of the items.

    iv.   Find the cumulative consumption values of the items.

    v.   Group the parts into three groups based on the following guide lines.

1.   A items: Items corresponding to top 70% of the annual consumption value of the items.

2.   **'B'** items: Items corresponding to next 20% of the annual consumption value of the items form top.

3.   **'C'** items: Items corresponding to 10% of the annual consumption value of the

items at the end.

6.5   PRODUCTION SCHEDULING

As already stated, production scheduling prepares a calendar to schedule different jobs on a set of machines in a shop floor. The appropriate use of tools and techniques by recognizing the types of scheduling problem will decrease the cycle time of production of each and every product as well as maximize the utilization of the machines and other manufacturing facilities, which are engaged in the business.

6.5.1 Types of Scheduling

The types of scheduled that exists in manufacturing are as given below.

 i. Single machine scheduling problem
 ii. Flow shop scheduling problem
 iii. Job shop scheduling problem

Single Machine Scheduling Problem

Single machine scheduling is broken down into problems with a single machine and machines running in parallel. The single machine scheduling problem with identical parallel machines and nonidentical parallel machines are two further classifications of the single machine scheduling problem with parallel machines.

Additionally, there is a single machine scheduling problem with uniform parallel machines and a single machine scheduling problem with unrelated parallel machines for the single machine scheduling problem with non-identical parallel machines.

Let t_{ij} represent the time it takes for the machine i to do the job j, where $i = 1, 2, 3$, etc., and $j = 1, 2, 3$, etc.

The following definitions describe the three categories of single machine scheduling problem with parallel machines.

1) The problem is referred to as identical parallel machines scheduling, if $t_{ij} = t_{1j}$ for all i and j.
This indicates that the speeds of all the parallel machines are the same. Each of the parallel machines will process each job in the same amount of time.

2) The problem is known as uniform parallel machines scheduling problem if $t_{ij} = t_{1j}/s_i$ for all I and j.

Here, s_i denotes the speed of machine i while t_{1j} denotes the amount of time it took machine 1 to process job j.

As a result, the parallel machines will operate at various speeds. For the parallel machines $1, 2, 3, …, m$ we assume $s_1, s_2, s_3, …, s_m$, respectively, with assumption being that $s_1 < s_2 < s_3 < … < s_m$.

The machine 1 is the one that works the slowest, and the machine m is the fastest machine.

For a given job, its processing times on the parallel machines will be as per the following relation: $1/s_1 > 1/s_2 > 1/s_3 > \ldots > 1/s_m$

3) The problem is referred to as an unrelated parallel machine scheduling problem, if tij is random for all i and j.

The processing times of a job on the parallel machines won't be correlated in this form of scheduling. This might be a result of the machines' varied technological capabilities, the jobs' various requirements, etc.

The single machine scheduling problem with single processor has the following measures of performance [Panneerselvam (2022) and Panneerselvam, Senthilkumar and Sivasankaran (2020)].

    i.   Minimizing mean flow time
    ii.   Minimizing weighted mean flow time
    iii.   Minimizing maximum lateness
    iv.   Minimizing mean tardiness
    v.   Minimizing number of tardy jobs.

The minimization of mean flow time of the single machine scheduling problem with single processor is minimized using Shortest Processing Time (SPT) rule.

The minimization of the weighted mean flow time is minimized using weighted shortest processing time (W-SPT) rule.

The maximum lateness is minimized using Earliest Due Date (EDD) rule.

One can use branch and bound technique to minimize the total tardiness of the single machine scheduling problem with single processor.

Hodgson's algorithm minimizes the number of tardy jobs of the single machine scheduling problem with single processor.

Flow Shop Scheduling

The flow shop scheduling problem has *n* independent jobs and *m* machines. Each job has a process sequence with *m* operations and further all the jobs have the same process sequence. The dominant measure of performance of this scheduling is the minimization of makespan of scheduling *n* independent jobs on *m* different machines.

Job Shop Scheduling

Job shop scheduling problem consists of *n* independent jobs and *m* different operations. The operation sequences of the jobs are heterogeneous. The dominant measure of performance of this problem is also minimization of the makespan of scheduling *n* independent jobs on *m* different machines.

6.5.2 Flow Shop Scheduling

The assumptions of the flow shop scheduling problem are given below.

    i. n independent jobs are available at the start of the scheduling.

    ii. m different machines are available from time 0.

    iii.   The process sequence is the same for all the jobs.

    iv.   The process time of each operation of each job is known at time zero.

    v.   The setup time of each operation of each job is included in the total processing time of that operation of the job at that machine

The dominant measure of performance of the flow shop scheduling problem is minimizing the makespan of scheduling n jobs on m machines. The makespan is the total elapsed time of completing all the jobs in the given batch.

6.5.2.1 Johnson's Algorithm for 2 Machines and n Jobs Problem

As stated already, the minimization of the makespan of scheduling n jobs on n different machines is of prime importance in the flow shop scheduling problem. This can be achieved through Johnson's algorithm for a special problem with 2 machines and n jobs, whose format is shown in Table 6. 7. In this table, t_{ij} is the processing time of the job i on the machine j, where i varied from 1 to n and j varies from 1 to m.

Table 6.7 Data Format of 2 Machines and n jobs Flow Shop Problem

Job i	Machine j	
	1	2
1	t_{11}	t_{12}
2	t_{21}	t_{22}
3	t_{31}	t_{32}
.		
.		
i	t_{i1}	t_{i2}
.		
n	t_{n1}	t_{n2}

Steps of Johnson's Algorithm

The steps of John's algorithm are as presented below.

Step1: Identify the least processing time among all the (undeleted) times irrespective of the jobs and machines in the Table 6.7.

    Note: When this step is executed for the first time, all the times are undeleted. As we progress to execute the steps, the times will be deleted in stages.

Step 2: Initially , n positions in the process sequence are empty.

Step 3: Check whether this least time lies on the machine 1 column or machine 2 column. If it is on the machine 1 column, then assign the corresponding job in the left most available position in the sequence; otherwise, assign the corresponding job in the right most available position in the sequence.

Step 4: Then delete the corresponding row in the Table 6.7.

Step 5: Repeat the Step 3 and Step 4 until all the jobs are assigned to the positions in the sequence.

Step 6: Draw a Gantt chart as per process sequence determined using the Steps 3 to 5 and find the makespan, which is the completion time of the last job on the machine 2.

Example 6.6

Consider the two machines and six jobs flow shop problem as shown in Table 6.8. Find the sequence of jobs, which minimizes the makespan using Johnson's algorithm.

Table 6.8 Data of Two Machines and Six Jobs Flow Shop Problem

Job	Machine 1	Machine 2
1	5	7
2	10	8
3	8	13
4	9	7
5	6	11
6	12	10

Solution.

The data of the given problem are reproduced in Table 6.9.

Table 6.9 Reproduction of Data of Table 6.8

Job	Machine 1	Machine 2
1	5	7
2	10	8
3	8	13
4	9	7
5	6	11
6	12	10

The application of the steps of the Johnson's algorithm is shown in Table 6.10 and the corresponding allocations of the jobs to different positions in the sequence are shown in Table 6.11. The process sequence obtained using the Johnson's algorithm is given below.

1-5-3-6-4-2

The Gantt chart for the above sequence of jobs is shown in Fig.6.11. The shaded potion in the Fig.6.11 corresponds to idle time. From this figure, it is observed that the makespan is 61 units of time.

Table 6.10 Applications of Johnson's Algorithm to Data in Table 6.8

Job	Machine 1	Machine 2
1	5 X	7 X
2	10 X	**8 X**
3	**8 X**	13 X
4	9 X	7 X
5	6 X	11 X
6	12	10

Table 6.11 Sequence of Jobs

Position in the séquence	1	2	3	4	5	6
Job séquence	1	5	3	6	2	4

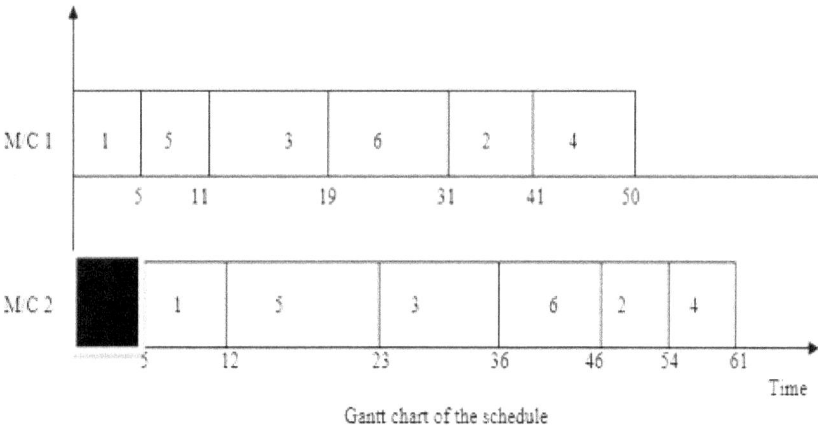

Fig.6.11 Gantt Chart of Example 6.6

6.5.2.2 Extension of Johnson's Algorithm for 3 Machines and *n* Jobs Problem

In the flow shop scheduling problem, if the number of machines is 3 and the number of jobs is *n*, the steps of the Johnson's algorithm will not yield optimal makespan as such. Hence, the steps of the algorithm are modified as under.

Step 1: Find the modified data of the problem to create Pseudo problem with 2 machines and n jobs.

Step 1.1: For the first operation of each job of the pseudo problem, add the processing times of that job on the machine 1 and the machine 2 of the real problem and treat it as its time.

Step 1.2: For the second operation of each job of the pseudo problem, add the processing times of that job on the machine 2 and the machine 3 and treat it as its time.

Step 2: Apply the steps of the Johnson's algorithm to the pseudo data with 2 machines and *n* jobs and find the process sequence, which will yield optimal makespan.
Step 3: Draw a Gantt chart using original data for the 3 machines and *n* jobs problem for the process sequence obtained in the Step 2 and find the optimal makespan,

.

Note: One can extend the steps of the Johnson's algorithm to 3 machines and *n* jobs flow shop scheduling problem, if at least one of the following two conditions is satisfied,

    i.   The minimum of the times of the jobs on the machine 1 is more than or equal to the maximum of the times of the jobs on the machine 2.
    ii.   The minimum of the times of the jobs on the machine 3 is more than or equal to the maximum of the times of the jobs on the machine 2.

If both the conditions are not satisfied, it is not possible to extend the Johnson's algorithm to 3 machines and *n* jobs flow shop problem.

One can use branch and bound algorithm to obtain the sequence of jobs for any problem with three or more machines and *n* jobs to minimize the makespan.

Example 6.7

Consider the 3 machines and 5 jobs flow shop problem shown in Table 6.12. Check whether Johnson's rule can be extended to this problem. If so, what is the optimal schedule and the corresponding makespan?

Table 6.12 Data of Example 6.7

Job	Machine 1	Machine 2	Machine 3
1	11	10	12
2	13	8	20
3	15	6	15
4	12	7	19
5	20	9	7

Solution

The data of Example 6.7 are reproduced in Table 6.13.

Table 6.13 Reproduction of Data of Example 6.7

Job	Machine 1	Machine 2	Machine 3
1	11	10	12
2	13	8	20
3	15	6	15
4	12	7	19
5	20	9	7

The pseudo problem with two machines and 5 jobs is shown in Table 6.14.

Table 6.14 Pseudo Problem of Data Shown in Table 6.13

Job	Pseudo Machine	
	Machine 1*	Machine 2*
1	21	22
2	21	28
3	21	21
4	19	26
5	29	16

Application of the Johnsons algorithm gives the following sequences of jobs for which the makespan is 92 units of time.

$$4-1-2-3-5 \ or \ 4-2-1-3-5$$

The Gantt chart for the sequence 4-1-2-3-5 is shown in Fig.6.12.

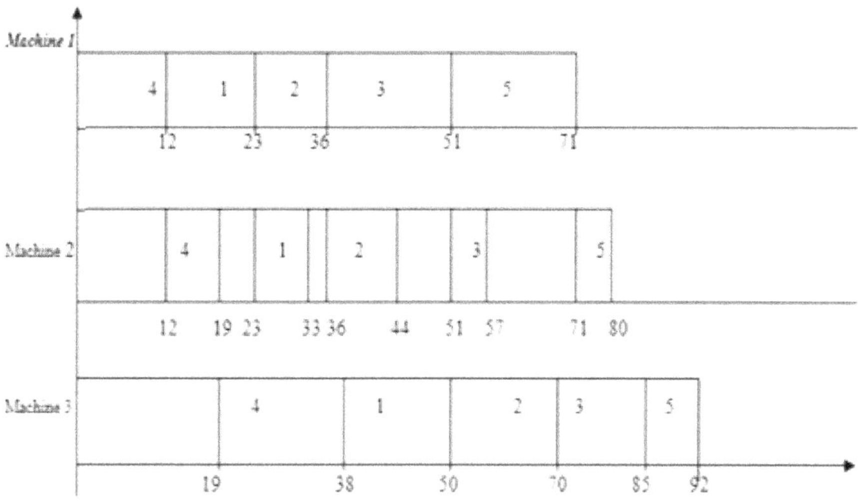

Fig.6.12 Gantt chart of Example 6.7 for sequence 4-1-2-3-5

REVIEW QUESTIONS

1. List the activities of process planning and control.

2. List the functions of production planning and control and also explain them in brief.

3. Distinguish between quantitative forecasting method and qualitative forecasting method. List the corresponding methods.

4. Explain the moving average method of forecasting using an example.

5. Explain the exponential smoothing method of forecasting using an example.

6. What is regression method? Explain the component of the simple regression.

7. What is production scheduling? Explain its functions.

8. Explain the objectives of materials management.

9. What are the functions of materials management.

10. Discuss the need for inventory control.

11. List and explain the functions of inventory control.

12. What are the types of inventories? Explain them.

13. Illustrate the aspect of economic order quantity model with a suitable graph.

14. A leading retail outlet plans for the economic order size of Air conditioner, which costs 40,000 rupees per unit. The annual demand for this product is 7,000 units. The ordering cost per order is Rs.6,000 and the carrying cost per unit per year is Rs.500. Determine the economic order quantity for the air conditioner.

15. The demand of washing machine in a retail shop is 10000 per year. The ordering cost per order is Rs.5000. The purchase price per unit of the TV is Rs.40,000. The lead time to deliver the items against the order is 3 weeks. The carrying cost per unit per year of the TV is 12% of its purchase price.

      i. Find the EOQ of the washing machine.

      ii. Find the ROL of the purchase model of inventory.

16. Distinguish between Q system of inventory and P system of inventory.

17. Discuss the needs of ABC analysis.

18. Illustrate the concept of ABC analysis using a suitable graph.

19. Give the steps of ABC analysis.

20. List the applications of ABC analysis.

21. Define production scheduling and list its types.

22. Discuss the following types of types of production scheduling problem.

    a. Single machine scheduling problem

    b. Flow shop scheduling problem

    c. Job shop scheduling problem

23. List and explain the assumptions of flow shop scheduling problem.

24. Give the steps of Johnson's algorithm to find the makespan of flow shop scheduling problem with 2 machines and n jobs.

25. Give the steps of extending Johnson's algorithm to find the makespan of flow shop scheduling problem with 3 machines and n jobs.

26. A flow shop problem contains 2 machines and 6 jobs. Obtain the optimal schedule and the corresponding makespan for this problem using Johnson's algorithm.

Job	Machine 1	Machine 2
1	6	7
2	10	6
3	8	12
4	10	7
5	7	11
6	12	13

27. A flow shop scheduling problem has 3 machines and 5 jobs. Check whether Johnson's rule can be extended to this problem. If at least one condition is satisfied, what is the optimal schedule and the corresponding makespan?

Job	Machine 1	Machine 2	Machine 3
1	7	4	3
2	9	5	8
3	5	1	7
4	6	2	5
5	10	3	4

CHAPTER 7 QUALITY CONTROL

7.1 INTRODUCTION

Manufacturing and service organizations produce items and offer services to clients, respectively. The company should concentrate on providing necessary quality within the given specification limits during this process. Consider the production of two-wheelers. The metrics for how well a two-wheeler is sold to clients are listed below.

- Actual mileage per litre of fuel realized is more than or equal to the promised minimum of mileage per litre.

- Time between consecutive breakdowns is more than the promised time.

- Average useful life of the two-wheeler is more than its promised economic life.

- Satisfaction of customers on journey comfort, while using the two-wheeler.

- Average annual cost of operation and maintenance of the two-wheeler is well below the promised cost by the company.

As a result, it is believed that a product's quality is a crucial feature that will affect customers' purchasing decisions. Additionally, happy consumers will have a multiplier impact in attracting new clients.

7.2 DEFINITION OF QUALITY

A product's ability to live up to expectations and be suitable for its intended uses is considered as its quality. If a product satisfies customers in terms of performance, product life, appearance, meeting the intended purpose, etc., it is said to be of high quality.

The product's compliance to the standard, which is defined in terms of tolerance limits with lower and upper specification limits, indicates how well it is made, which is known as quality. The tolerance limit is crucial, because no manufacturing process creates any product with exact dimensions, because of the limitations of machines, materials and workers. As a result, a specification-based allowed range is created for each and every dimension of the product or component, which is then approved by quality control or inspection.

7.3 CHARACTERISTICS OF QUALITY

The product has many quality characteristics, which are classified into variable characteristic and attribute characteristic. The variable quality characteristics of a product includes length, breadth and height of product with cuboid shape components, and diameter and length in the case of cylindrical component, etc. The attribute characteristics of quality of a product are "Good" or "Bad", "Accept" or 'Reject", "OK" or "Not OK", etc. The product has a wide range of desirable qualities, which can be divided into variable qualities and attribute qualities. The length, breadth, and height of a product with a cuboid shape, as well as the diameter and length of a cylindrical object, are examples of a product's variable quality attributes. The attributes that describe a product's quality are "Good" or "Bad," "Accept" or "Reject," "OK" or "Not OK," etc.

7.4 CONTROL CHART

It has already been mentioned that it is impossible to manufacture parts or products with exact measurements. Therefore, based on historical data, practitioners should create a control chart with a mean value that follows three sigma standards and lower and upper control limits.

A sample control chart is shown in Fig.7.1.

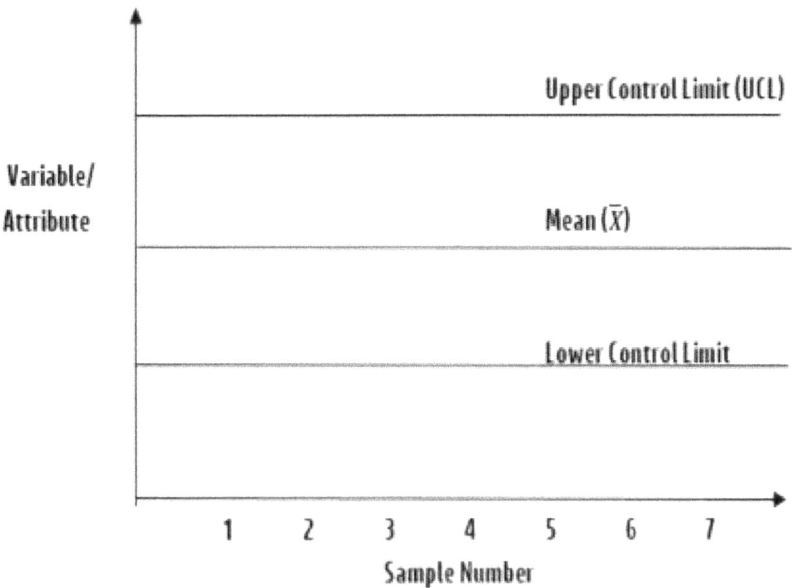

Fig.7.1 Sample control chart

The classification of quality control techniques is given in Fig.7.2.

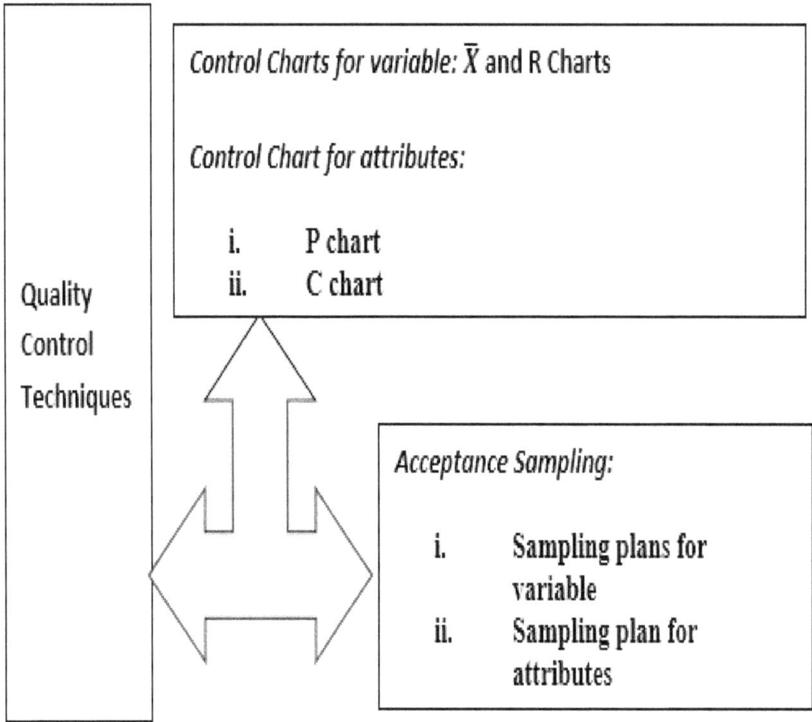

Fig. 7.2 Classification of quality control techniques

7.4.1 X Bar and R Charts

X bar and R charts are used jointly to control variable quality. X bar chart is based on the means of the recent most fixed number of samples taken, where as the R chart is based on the ranges of the recent most fixed number of samples. As the name of X bar indicates the control of mean characters of a variable of a product, it is called as mean chart, which shows the current status of the process in terms of mean quality. The R chart reveals the current quality status of a process based on the variations of the means of the observations of the samples.

In this pair of charts, k number of samples with n observations in each sample will be taken. Then X bar chart and R chart will be constructed to assess the current status of the process in terms of mean and variance of the observations.

The control limits of the X bar chart are as given below.

$$UCL_{\bar{x}} = \bar{\bar{X}} + A\bar{R}$$

$$LCL_{\bar{x}} = \bar{\bar{X}} - A\bar{R}$$

Where,

$UCL_{\bar{x}}$ is the upper control limit of $\bar{X}$

$LCL_{\bar{x}}$ is the lower control limit of $\bar{X}$

$\bar{\bar{X}}$ is the mean of the means of the samples

$\bar{R}$ is mean of the ranges of the samples

A is the mean factor as a function of sample size n as shown in Table 7.1.

The control limits of R chart are as given below.

$$UCL_R = BR$$
$$LCL_R = CR$$

Where,

UCL_R is the upper control limit of R

LCL_R is the lower control limit of R

B is the upper range factor as a function of sample size n as shown in Table 7.1

C is the lower range factor as a function of sample size n as shown in Table 7.1

Table 7.1 Data of Mean Factor, Upper Range Factor and Lower Range Factor

Sample Size n	Mean Factor A	Upper range Factor B	Lower Range Factor C
2	1.88	3.27	0.00
3	1.02	2.57	0.00
4	0.73	2.28	0.00
5	0.58	2.11	0.00
6	0.48	2.00	0.00
7	0.42	1.92	0.08
8	0.37	1.86	0.14
9	0.34	1.82	0.18
10	0.31	1.78	0.22
11	0.29	1.74	0.26
12	0.27	1.72	0.28
13	0.25	1.69	0.31
14	0.24	1.67	0.33
15	o.22	1.65	0.35
16	0.21	1.64	0.36
17	0.20	1.62	0.38
18	0.19	1.61	0.39
19	0.19	1.60	0.40
20	0.18	1.59	0.41

Example 7.1

The data in Table 7.2 were obtained over a 5-day period to indicate X bar and R control charts for a quality characteristic of a certain manufacturing product that had required a substantial amount of rework. All the figures apply to the product made on a single machine by a single operator. The sample size was 5. Two samples were taken per day. Comment on the process using X bar and R charts.

Table 7.2 Data of Samples for $\bar{X}$ and R Control Charts

Sample number	Observation				
	1	2	3	4	5
1	11	12	13	10	9
2	6	10	10	11	9
3	11	12	9	12	10
4	14	10	8	13	11
5	12	11	11	10	7
6	11	10	10	12	11
7	10	12	13	13	12
8	10	11	11	10	12
9	12	13	11	12	10
10	11	13	9	9	12

Solution.

Table 7.3 gives the data as shown in the Table 7.2 with additional calculations for X bar and R Control Charts.

Table 7.3 Data of $\bar{X}$ and R Control Charts with Calculations

Sample number	Observation					$\bar{X}$	R
	1	2	3	4	5		
1	11	12	13	10	9	11	4
2	6	10	10	11	9	9.2	5
3	11	12	9	12	10	10.8	3
4	14	10	8	13	11	11.2	6
5	12	11	11	10	7	10.2	5
6	11	10	10	12	11	10.8	2
7	10	12	13	13	12	12	3
8	10	11	11	10	12	10.8	2
9	12	13	11	12	10	11.6	3
10	11	13	9	9	12	10.8	4
					Total	108.4	37

The control limits of the X bar chart as given below.

$$UCL_{\bar{x}} = \bar{\bar{X}} + A\bar{R}$$

$$LCL_{\bar{x}} = \bar{\bar{X}} - A\bar{R}$$

Where,

$UCL_{\bar{x}}$ is the upper control limit of $\bar{X}$

$LCL_{\bar{x}}$ is the lower control limit of $\bar{X}$

$\bar{\bar{X}}$ is the mean of the means of the samples

$\bar{R}$ is mean of the ranges of the samples

A is the mean factor as a function of sample size n as shown in Table 7.1.

$$\bar{\bar{X}} = \frac{\sum_{i=1}^{10} \bar{X}_i}{k} = = \frac{108.4}{10} = 10.84, k \text{ is the number of samples}$$

$$\bar{R} = \frac{\sum_{i=1}^{10} R_i}{k} = \frac{37}{10} = 3.7, \text{where } k \text{ is the number of samples}$$

When n = 5, from the Table 7.1, A = 0.58, B = 2.11, C = 0

$$UCL_{\bar{x}} = \bar{\bar{X}} + A\bar{R} = 10.84 + 0.58 \times 3.7 = 12.986$$

$$UCL_{\bar{x}} = \bar{\bar{X}} + A\bar{R} = 10.84 - 0.58 \times 3.7 = 8.694$$

The control limits of R chart are as given below.

$$UCL_R = B\bar{R}$$

$$LCL_R = C\bar{R}$$

Where,

UCL_R is the upper control limit of R

LCL_R is the lower control limit of R

B is the upper range factor as a function of sample size n as shown in Table 7.1

C is the lower range factor as a function of sample size n as shown in Table 7.1

$$UCL_R = B\bar{R} = 2.11 \times 3.7 = 7.807$$

$$LCL_R = C\bar{R} = 0 \times 3.7 = 0$$

The control charts for $\bar{X}$ and R are shown 7.3 and Fig.7.4, respectively. It is observed that the points in the $\bar{X}$ chart as well as in the R chart are within the respective control limits.

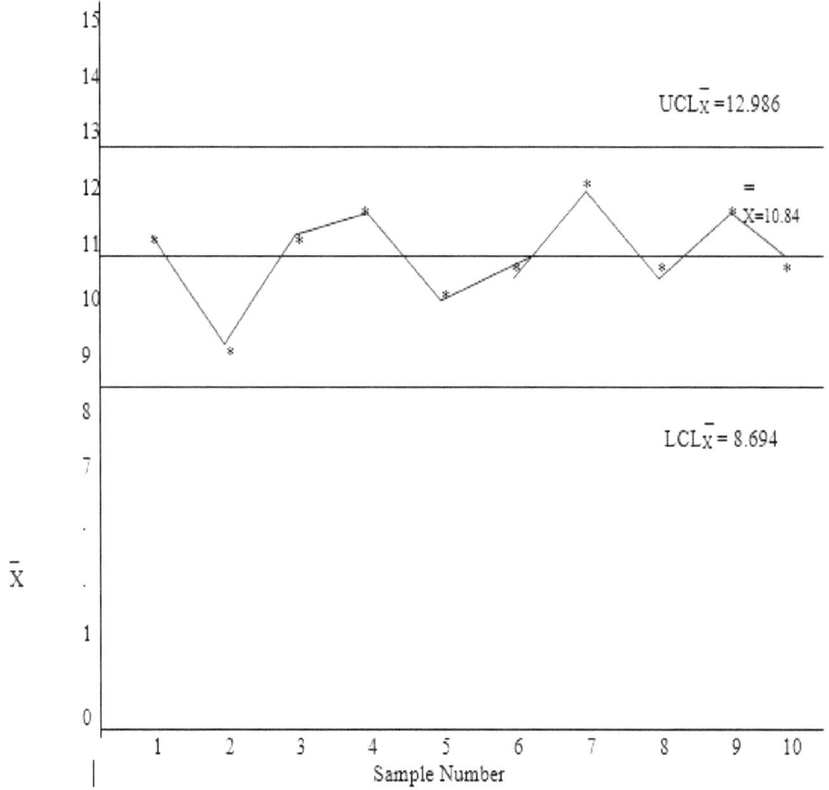

Fig.7.3 Plot of X bar chart

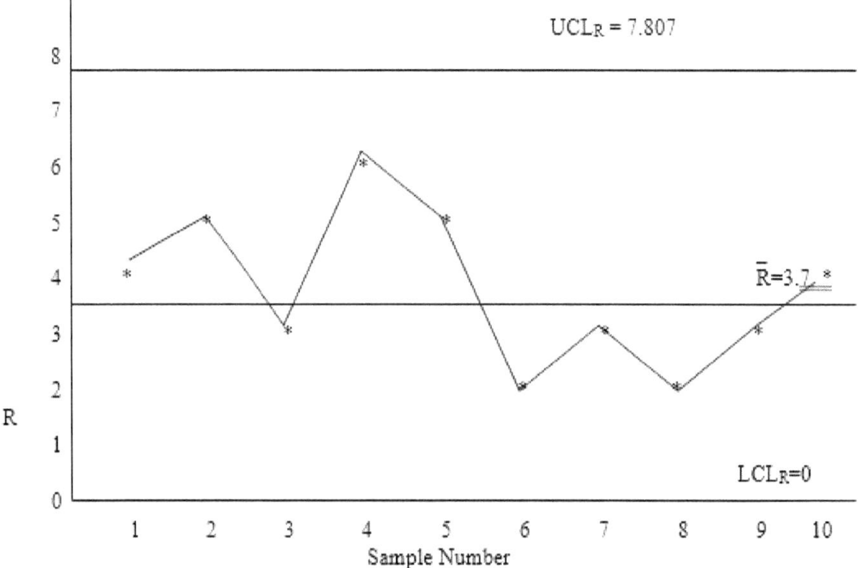

Fig.7.4 Plot of R chart

7.4.2 *P* Chart (Percent Defective Chart)

P chart is a percent defective chart, which is applied in a situation where each and every piece in the sample with *n* pieces is inspected and then the defective pieces are rejected. This clearly shows the attribute nature of the data of the inspection of the units in the sample. In each sample, the value of *P* is given by the following formula.

$$P_i = \frac{Number\ of\ defective\ pieces\ in\ the\ smaple\ i\ (d_i)}{Sample\ size}$$

The mean of percent defective is as computed below.

$$\bar{p} = \frac{\sum_{i=1}^{k} p_i}{n \times k}$$

Where,

  k is the number of samples

  n is the sample size

  $\bar{P}$ is the mean of percent defective

  P_i is the percent defective of the sample I, I = 1, 2, 3, ..., k

  The control limits of the *P* chart are given below.

$$UCL_p = \bar{p} + 3 \times \sqrt{\left(\frac{\bar{p} \times (1 - \bar{p})}{n}\right)}$$

$$LCL_p = \bar{p} - 3 \times \sqrt{\left(\frac{\bar{p} \times (1 - \bar{p})}{n}\right)}$$

Where,

  UCL_p is the upper control limit of *P* chart.

  LCL_p is the lower control limit of *P* chart

  n is the sample size

  $\bar{P}$ is the mean of percent defective

Example 7.2

Alpha electronic company manufactures cathode ray tubes on mass production basis. At some intermediate point of production line, 10 samples of size 25 each have been taken. Tubes within each sample were classified into good or bad. The related data are given in Table 7.4 Construct a suitable control chart with 3 sigma limit and comment on the process.

Table 7.4 Data of Good and Bad of Cathode Ray Tubes

Sample number	1	2	3	4	5	6	7	8	9	10
No. of defective tubes	4	10	2	3	6	5	2	4	3	2

Solution.

The given data of Example 7.2 are given in Table 7.5 with additional details.

Table 7.5 Data of Table 7.4 with Additional Details

Sample number, i	1	2	3	4	5	6	7	8	9	10
No. of defective tubes, d_i	4	10	2	3	6	5	2	4	3	2
Percent defective, p_i	0.16	0.40	0.08	0.12	0.24	0.20	0.08	0.16	0.12	0.08

$\bar{P} = \frac{\sum_{i=1}^{k} P_i}{n \times k}$, where n = 25 and k = 10. The values of p_i, I = 1, 2, 3, . . ., 10 are shown in the Table 7.5.

$$\bar{p} = \frac{\sum_{i=1}^{k} P_i}{n \times k} = \frac{41}{25 \times 10} = 0.164$$

The formulas for upper control limit and lower control limit for P_i are given below.

$$UCL_p = \bar{p} + 3 \times \sqrt{\left(\frac{\bar{p} \times (1 - \bar{p})}{n}\right)}$$

$$LCL_p = \bar{p} - 3 \times \sqrt{\left(\frac{\bar{p} \times (1 - \bar{p})}{n}\right)}$$

Where,

UCL_p is the upper control limit of P chart.

LCL_p is the lower control limit of P chart

n is the sample size

$\bar{P}$ is the mean of percent defective

$$UCL_P = \bar{P} + 3 \times \sqrt{\left(\frac{\bar{P} \times (1 - \bar{P})}{n}\right)}$$

$$= 0.164 + 3 \times \sqrt{\left(\frac{0.164 \times (1 - 0.164)}{25}\right)} = 0.386$$

$$LCL_p = \bar{P} - 3 \times \sqrt{\left(\frac{\bar{P} \times (1 - \bar{P})}{n}\right)}$$

$$= 0.164 - 3 \times \sqrt{\left(\frac{0.164 \times (1 - 0.164)}{25}\right)} = -\,-\,-\,0.058$$

$$\cong \quad 0 \text{ (since, negative value is not possible)}$$

The *P* chart of this example is shown in Fig.7.5.

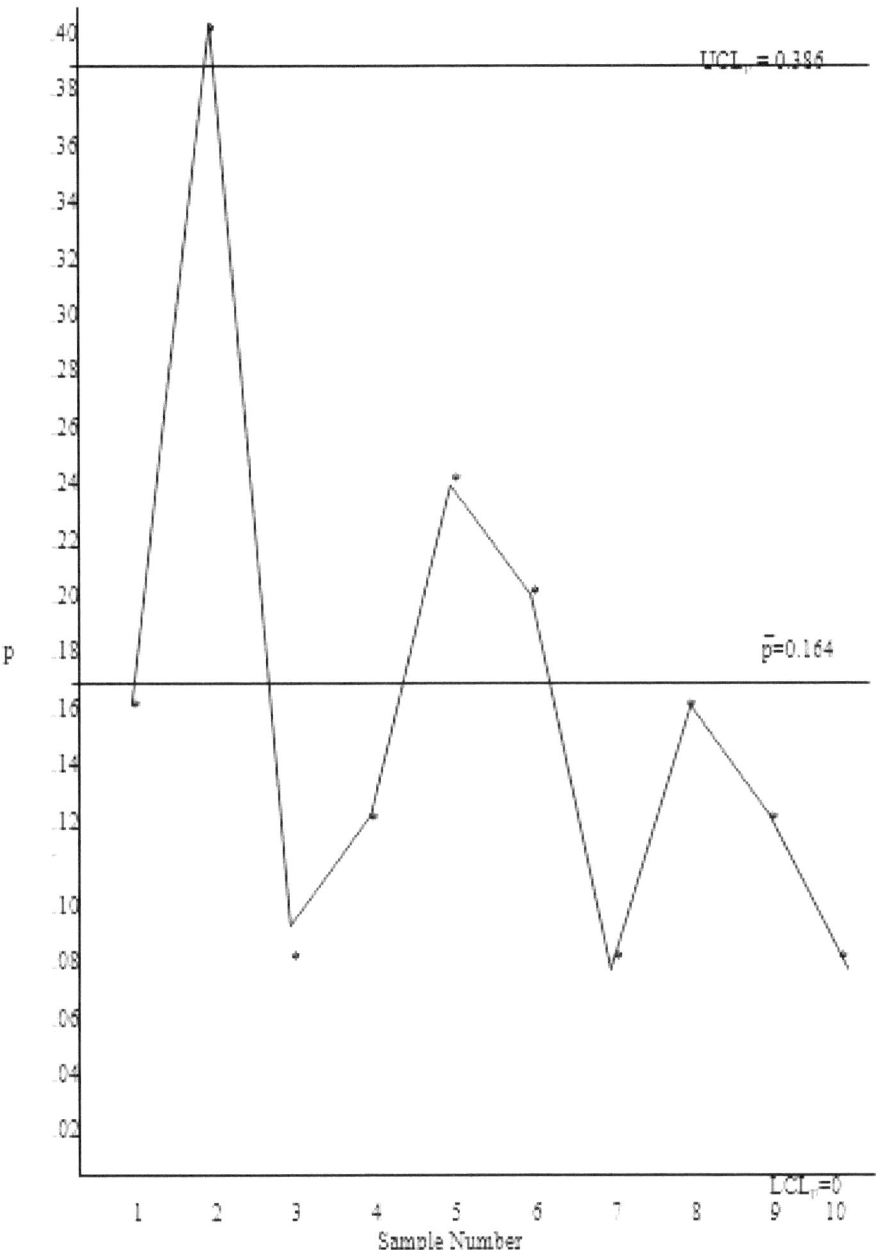

Fig.7.5 Plot of *P* chart of Example 7.2

Comment: With the exception of the second sample, every point on the control chart is inside the acceptable range. There is no need for any correction to have control because the points relative to samples 3 to 10 are comfortably within the control boundaries.

7.4.3 C Chart

C chart comes under attribute control chart. This resembles a *P* chart; however, the sample size is only one. This is relevant in cases where a casting is formed and the quantity of surface flaws should be kept under control. It is possible to forget to add a certain component when assembling a product. To control such undesirable incidents, C chart is used.

$$\bar{C} = \frac{Sum\ of\ all\ defects\ occured\ in\ all\ samples}{Sample\ size\ \times Number\ of\ smaples} = \frac{\sum_{i=1}^{k} d_i}{n \times k}$$

Where,

$\bar{C}$ is the overall mean of the defects

k is the number of samples

n is the sample size, which is 1 for C chart

d_i is the number of defects in the sample i, i = 1, 2, 3, . . . , k

The formulas for the control limits of this chart are as under.

$$UCL_C = \bar{C} + 3\sqrt{\bar{C}}$$

$$LCL_C = \bar{C} - 3\sqrt{\bar{C}}$$

Where,

UCL_C is the upper control limit of the C chart

LCL_C is the lower control limit of the C chart

$\bar{C}$ is the overall mean of the defects

Example 7.3

The following Table 7.6 gives the number of missing rivets noted in a newly fabricated car. Construct a suitable control chart for the given data and comment on the process.

Table 7.6 Data of Number of Defects of Samples

Car number	1	2	3	4	5	6	7	8	9	10
Number of missing rivets	10	12	18	15	9	20	11	10	16	8

Solution

The data shown in the Table 7.6 are reproduced in Table 7.7.

Table 7.7 Data of Number of Defects of Samples

Car number	1	2	3	4	5	6	7	8	9	10
Number of missing rivets	10	12	18	15	9	20	11	10	16	8

$$\bar{C} = \frac{Sum\ of\ all\ defects\ occured\ in\ all\ samples}{Sample\ size\ \times Number\ of\ smaples} = \frac{\sum_{i=1}^{k} d_i}{n \times k} = \frac{129}{1 \times 10} = 12.9$$

$$UCL_C = \bar{C} + 3\sqrt{\bar{C}} = 12.9 + 3 \times \sqrt{12.9} = 23.68 \ = \ 24\ (approx.)$$

$$LCL_C = \bar{C} - 3\sqrt{\bar{C}} = 12.9 - 3 \times \sqrt{12.9} = 2.12 \ = \ 2\ (approx.)$$

The C-Chart of this problem is shown in Fig.7.6.
Remark: All the points are within the control limits.

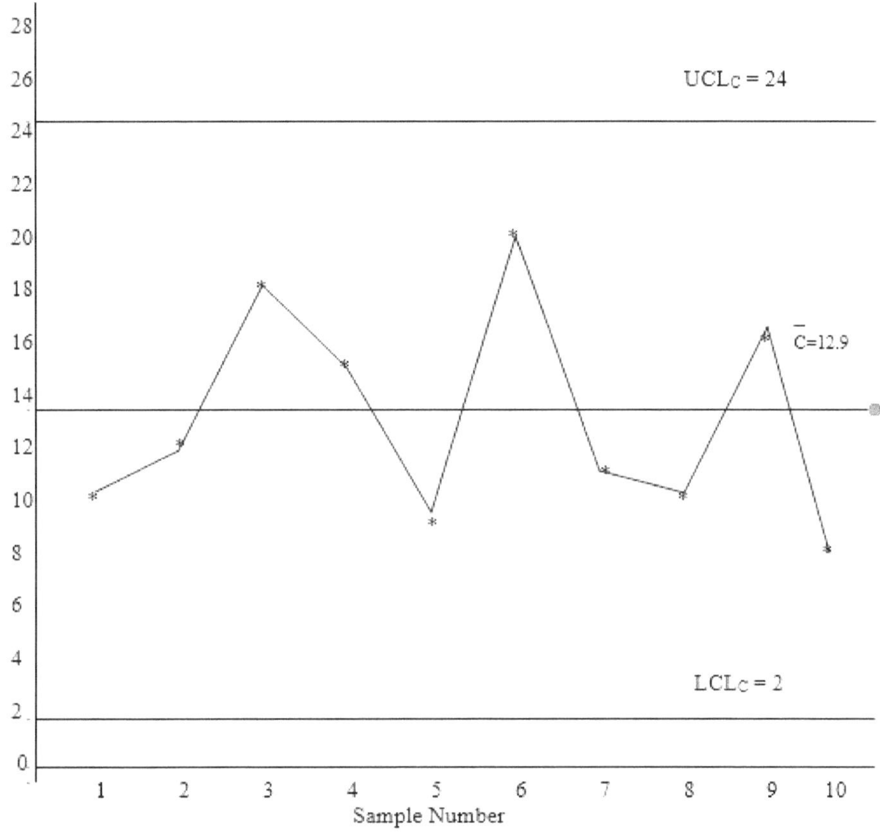

Fig.7.6 Plot of C chart of Example 7.3

7.5 ACCEPTANCE SAMPLING

The perfect quality can be installed in products through 100% inspection, which has the following drawbacks.

i.   It is not feasible in destructive testing.
ii. It is time consuming, because every piece in the lot is inspected to find whether it is defective or not.
iii. It introduces monotonous effect on the quality assistants in industries.

Hence, an alternative to 100% inspection is sampling, which is called as acceptance sampling. This is the process of checking the quality of a lot through sample result.

In the acceptance sampling, only the pieces in the sample are inspected to find the number of defective pieces in it. Then, based on this result, a judgment will be taken to decide whether the lot is to be accepted or not. Though, the sampling introduces comfort of making decision quickly, it is associated with two types of errors, viz. Type 1 error and Type 2 error.

Type 1 Error: This error is also known as producer's risk, which is denoted by alpha. It is the probability of rejecting a good lot.

Type 2 Error: This error is also known as consumer's risk, which is denoted by beta. It is the probability of accepting a bad lot.

In reality, it is very difficult to avoid both errors. Hence, based on a meaningful combination of producer's risk (Alpha), Consumer's risk (Beta), Acceptable Quality level (AQL) and Lot Tolerance Percent Defective (LTPD) decided by the buyer and producer, a sampling plan will be designed to find the sample size (n) and acceptance number (C).

These are characterized in Fig.7.7, which is known as Operating Characteristic (OC) curve.

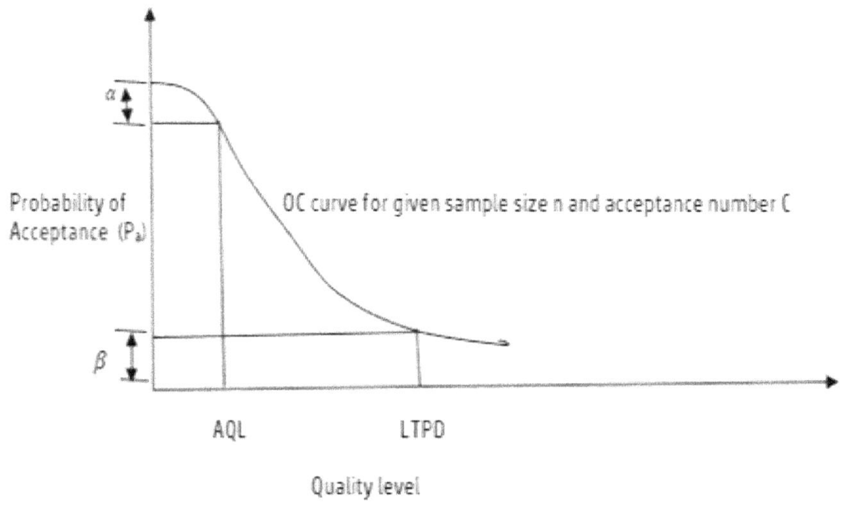

Fig.7.7 Operating Characteristic (OC) curve

In the Fig.7.7, the producer's risk and consumer's risk have been already defined. AQL is the acceptable quality level, which means that the corresponding probability of acceptance is agreeable to both parties. Similarly, LTPD is the extreme point beyond which the quality of the lot will be bad. The quality level in between AQL and LTPD belongs to indifference zone.

7.5.1 Steps of Single Sampling Plan

The single sampling plan aims to judge the quality of the lot either to accept or reject based on a sample characteristic, whose steps are as listed below.

Step 1: Input the following.

- Lot size (N)
- Producer's risk (Alpha)
- Consumer's risk (Beta)

- Acceptable Quality level (*AQL*)
- Lot Tolerance Percent Defective (*LTPD*)

Step 2: Find the sample size (n) and acceptance number *C*.

Step 3: Select a sample of size n and inspect all the pieces in it to find the number of defective pieces (*d*).

Step 4: If the number of defectives (*d*) is less than or equal to the acceptance number *C*, then accept the lot; otherwise, reject the lot.

7.5.2 Steps of Double Sampling Plan

The double sampling plan aims to judge the quality of the lot either to accept or reject it based on the characters of two samples, whose steps are as listed below.

Step 1: Input the following.

- Lot size (*N*)
- Producer's risk (Alpha)
- Consumer's risk (Beta)
- Acceptable Quality level (*AQL*)
- Lot Tolerance Percent Defective (*LTPD*)

Step 2: Find the following.
Sample size of first sample (n_1)
Sample size of the second sample (n_2)
First acceptance number C_1.
Second acceptance number C_2.

Step 3: Select first sample of size n_1 and inspect all the pieces in it to find the number of defective pieces (d_1) in it.

Step 4: If the number of defectives (d_1) of the first sample is less than or equal to the acceptance number C_1, then accept the lot and go Step 7; else go to Step 5.

Step 5: Select second sample of size n_2 and inspect all the pieces in it to find the number of defective pieces (d_2) in it.

Step 6: If the sum of the number of defectives pieces in the first sample(d_1) and that in the second sample (d_2) is less than or equal to the acceptance number $C2$, then accept the lot; otherwise reject the lot.

Step 7: Continue from Step 3 to Step 6 at a predetermined time of the shift.

REVIEW QUESTIONS

1. Define quality.
2. List and explain the metrics of quality.
3. Distinguish between quality characteristics.
4. Explain the elements of control chart with a suitable graph.

5. Give the classification of quality control techniques.
6. Discuss the objective of X bar chart and R chart along with their control limits.
7. The information in the following table was gathered over the course of five days in order to show an X bar and R control chart for a quality attribute of a specific manufactured product that had necessitated a significant amount of rework. The data pertains to the item produced by a single operator using a single machine. The number of samples was 10. Every day, two samples were collected. The sample size is 3. Explain the procedure using the X bar and R charts and comment on the process.

Sample number	Observation		
	1	2	3
1	13	12	11
2	8	10	9
3	11	10	9
4	10	12	8
5	8	12	11
6	11	9	8
7	10	11	12
8	10	11	12
9	12	10	11
10	10	11	7

8. Discuss the objective of P chart along with their control limits.
9. Resistors are mass produced by the Beta Electronics Company. There have been taken ten samples, each of size 100, at some intermediate step in the production line. Each sample's resistors were categorized as either good or bad. The following table contains the pertinent information. Create a P-chart with a 3-sigma limit and provide feedback on the procedure.

Sample number	1	2	3	4	5	6	7	8	9	10
No. of defective resistors	10	12	18	111	12	21	12	9	10	7

10. Discuss the objective of C chart along with their control limits.
11. The quantity of flaws in a casting used to create the crank case of a diesel engine is shown in the following table. Construct a C – chart with 3-sigma limits and comment on the casting process.

Casting No. (i)	1	2	3	4	5	6	7	8	9	10
Number of defects (C_i)	12	10	20	12	11	18	14	11	15	12

12. What is sampling plan? Discuss its importance.
13. Distinguish between 100% inspection and acceptance sampling.
14. Distinguish between producer's risk and consumer's risk.
15. Give the sketch of OC curve and explain its parameters.
16. Give the steps of single sampling plan.
17. Give the steps of double sampling plan,

CHAPTER 8 MANAGEMENT CONCEPTS

8.1 INTRODUCTION

It is challenging to define management because there isn't a single, widely agreed term. On the other hand, a straightforward classical definition describes it as the "skill of getting things done by others." This definition has two components: achieving goals and directing group actions in that direction. The art of management is knowing what has to be done and making sure it is done as effectively as possible. The method through which a cooperative organization directs activity toward shared goals is called management. All resources must be coordinated through the processes of planning, organizing, staffing, directing, and controlling in order to achieve set objectives.

8.2 NATURE OF MANAGEMENT

The management can be thought of the following natures.
- Management as an art
- Management as a science

Management as an Art: Managers develop experience by applying their management skills consistently and taking on new challenges. More talents and abilities for applying knowledge to practice are developed as a result.

Management as a Science: The fundamentals of management can be applied to any kind of organization in the ambit of science, which is governed by a set of rules/ principles. It adheres to certain scientific tenets.

8.3 LEVELS OF MANAGEMENT

The decision-making situations arise in three different levels of management, which are as listed below.

i. Top level management
ii. Middle level management
iii. Bottom level management

Top Level Management

The board of directors, the CEO, and/or the managing director make up the top-level management. The senior management oversees an organization's goals and policies and is the ultimate source of authority. It spends more time in coordinating and planning tasks.

Middle Level Management

Middle level managers include branch managers and departmental managers. For the operation of their departments, they answer to top management. They spend more time in performing organizational and guiding tasks.

Low Level Management

The term "lower level" refers to the operational or supervisory levels of management. Supervisors, foremen, section officers, superintendents, etc. make up this group. Supervisory management, "refers to those executives whose work needs to be primarily with personal oversight and direction of operational staff". In other words, they are focused on the managerial function of direction and control.

8.4 FUNCTIONS OF MANAGEMENT

Functions of management is classified into five types, which are as presented below.

    i.   Planning
    ii.   Organizing
    iii.   Staffing
    iv.   Directing
    v.   Controlling

Planning Function

A plan in an organization means a set of future courses of actions. It is a decision-making and problem-solving exercise. Choosing a course of action to accomplish desired goals is planning. Planning is therefore the deliberate consideration of methods and approaches to achieve predetermined goals of an organization such that the overall productivity is maximized.

Organizing Function

Organizing function in a firm is to supply all the resources necessary for its operation such as raw materials, equipment, capital and staff. Choosing and delivering both human and non-human resources to the organizational structure is part of the process of organizing a firm.

The following are included in the organising role of management as a process.

i. Identification of activities.

ii. Classification of activity groupings.

iii. Assigning the responsibilities to the employees at different levels of the organization chart.

iv.   The transfer of power and establishment of responsibility

v.   Coordinating the connections between power and responsibility.

Staffing Function

The management's staffing task entails the following.

- Manpower Scheduling
- Recruitment, Selection & Placement
- Training & Development
- Remuneration
- Performance Evaluation
- Promotions and transfers

Direction Function

Directing is described as a procedure, which has the following tasks performed by managers.

- Giving instructions
- Providing guidance
- Monitor employee performance to meet predetermined objectives

The management process is stated to be at its core while directing.

Controlling Function

The controlling has following tasks.

1. Fixing standard performance
2. Assessing actual performance.
3. Comparison of actual performance with the standard performance to find deviation.
4. If deviation occurs, taking corrective action.

8.5 CONTRIBUTIONS OF MANAGEMENT GURUS

Scientific management aims to improve economic efficiency, particularly worker productivity. It was one of the first initiatives to use science in management and industrial engineering.

The contribution of F.W. Taylor and Hendry Fayol towards these principles are presented in this section.

8.5.1   F.W Taylor Contribution

Taylor saw that workers weren't working as productively as they could. And he believed that this situation was developing as a result of carelessness with regard to the waste.

Taylor focused on experiments at his place of employment to improve worker productivity so that the highest output might be obtained by applying the greatest amount of effort.

American engineer and inventor Frederick Winslow Taylor created the scientific management theory by applying his technical and scientific skills to management. Shop floor management (1903) and the principles of scientific management (1911) are his two most significant books supporting his theory.

The applications of the scientific management are a listed below.

i. Scientific management theory is significant since practically all industrial business operations throughout the world adopt its method of management.

ii. General business processes like planning, process design, quality control, cost accounting, and ergonomics are also affected by it.

iii. The practitioners will have a better understanding of industrial management because of their theoretical knowledge. Additionally, they learn how managers can utilize quantitative analysis, which is the study of numbers and other quantifiable data, to enhance the productivity of organization.

The elements of principles advocated by Taylor are as listed below.

    i. Setting scientific task
   ii. Differential payment system
  iii. Recognition of supervision
  iv. Scientific recruiting and training
   v. Economy
  vi. Mental revolution

Setting Scientific Task

Taylor believed that it is not possible to precisely know the tasks and their contents that the employees of an organization are ought to perform. The manager is responsible to decide the extent of work that should be allocated to each employee in each day. This aspect of performing a specific quantity of work in a day is called scientific task setting, which ensures a preset productivity of the organization.

Differential Payment System

Under this system, a worker would receive a piece rate benefit, which would entice them to work harder for higher pay. Additionally, more incentives would be implemented to raise the standardization of output, which would encourage workers to produce more, complete more tasks than they had previously, and make better use of downtime in order to increase their pay.

Reorganization of Supervision

According to Taylor, the employees should only put emphasis on preparing or performing. There should be eight foremen, including four for planning and four for carrying out. They had the roles of route clerk, instruction card clerk, time and cost clerk, and disciplinarian for planning, and speed boss, gang boss, repair boss, and inspector for carrying out.

Scientific Recruiting and Training

Employees and staff should be chosen and hired using scientific principles. Every employee should be developed and trained by management by giving them the right information and instruction to improve their skills and make them more productive. This in turn will improve the organizational productivity.

Economy

To control costs and comprehensively decrease and ultimately eliminate waste, an effective cost accounting system should be used. This system helps to record facts and figures in a desired accounting format and then facilitates to analyze several ratios to effect better control on all performance measures.

Mental Revolution

Taylor stated that instead of fighting over profits and perks, management and employees should endeavor to understand one another in order to maximize output, profit, and benefits. This approach helps to improve synergy among the employees, which will lead to increase in harmony among them and increase in the productivity of the organization.

The principles of Taylor are presented below.

- Use the scientific method to analyse work and identify the most effective technique to do particular tasks rather than working by rule of thumb.
- Match workers to their jobs based on their capabilities and motivation instead assigning them randomly to the jobs to have best results.
- The supervisor should have close observation of employees' performance in terms of whether they follow all the instructions and work towards efficient and effective output.
- The workload among the managers and employees should be divided such that the managers spend their time towards planning and training, whereas the employees concentrate on carrying out their jobs efficiently and effectively for better productivity.

8.5.2 Hendry Fayol Contributions

The fourteen principles of Hendry Fayol are as listed below.

    i.   Division of work
   ii.   Authority

    iii. Discipline
    iv. Unity of command
    v. Unity of direction
    vi. Subordination of individual interest to general interest
    vii. Remuneration
    viii. Centralization
    ix. Scalar chain
    x. Order
    xi. Equity
    xii. Stability Of Tenure of Personnel
    xiii. Initiative
    xiv. Espirit De Corps

i.   **Division Of Work**: To guarantee that effort and attention are concentrated on specific aspects of the task, work should be divided among individuals and groups. The best approach to utilize the organization's people resources, according to Fayol, is through work specialization.

ii.   **Authority**: Responsibility and authority share many similarities. Fayol advocated authority as having the right to issue commands and the ability to demand compliance. Since responsibility requires taking accountability, authority is inherently linked to it. The person who has responsibility also assured authority.

iii.   **Discipline**: The employees in an organization should work in integrated manner for the success of the organization. The employee who deviates from the common goal can be shown a kind of penalization to pull him back to the main stream of work towards achieving the common goal of the organization.

iv.   **Unity of Command**: Unity of command ensures that a subset of workers receive commands from only one manager/ superior.

v.   **Unity of Direction**: Unity of direction aims to take the entire organization towards a common objective in a unified direction.

vi.   **Subordination of Individual Interests to General Interests**: The interest of every individual employee in an organization should align with interest of the organization.

vii.   **Remuneration**: According to this notion, workers need to receive fair compensation for the labor they perform. Underpaying employees makes it difficult for businesses to retain high-caliber staff members and keep them motivated. This compensation should comprise both monetary and non-monetary incentives. A system for rewarding good performance should also be in place to inspire personnel.

viii.   **Centralization**: Centralization according to Fayol is the reduction of the significance of the subordinate position. Decentralization is becoming more significant in recent times with a view to have close control. Depending on the particular organization the manager is working for, either centralization or decentralization should be implemented to varying degrees.

ix.   **Scalar Chain:** In hierarchies, managers form links in a chain-like authority scale. Every manager, from the president to the first line manager, has a certain level of authority. The President has the most power, whereas the first-line manager has the least. Upper-level managers should always be apprised of the work that lower-level managers are doing. A scalar chain must exist and it must be followed if the organization is to succeed.

x.   **Order:** All resources and personnel connected to a certain type of activity should be handled as equally as possible for the benefit of efficiency and coordination.

xi.   **Equity**: Equity gives importance to treat all employees as equally as possible.

xii.   **Stability of Tenure of Personnel**: Management should constantly place a high focus on keeping productive staff. Hiring new employees is typically accompanied by higher rates of product rejection as well as recruitment and selection expenses. Further, retaining employees for longer tenure will poster good image of the company in the employment market, which will motivate meritorious applicants to apply for positions in the organization.

xiii.   **Initiative**: Management should encourage the initiatives of employees, which are characterized as new or extra job activities carried out through their self-direction.

xiv.   **Espirit De Corps**: Management should promote harmony and positive attitudes among the workforce.

8.5.3 Comparison of F.W Taylor and Hendry Fayol Theories of Management

Henry Fayol and F.W. Taylor made contributions to management science. Both of these pioneers' works have aspects that are comparable to and different from one another. Both approached this issue using the scientific method. The fact that Taylor focused on the operational level and worked up the industrial ladder, while Fayol focused on the top management and worked down in the hierarchy.

The similarities of Taylor's principle of management and Hendry Fayol principles of management are presented below.

i. They both saw how management is a worldwide concept.
ii. Both used scientific approaches to address management-related issues.
iii. Both individuals recognised the value of staff and their management at all levels.
iv. Both desired to enhance the management techniques.

v. Both of them used real-world experience to create their concepts.

vi. They both provided explanations of their concepts in their works.

vii.They both emphasised the importance of employers and employees working together.

The dissimilarities of Taylor's principle of management and Hendry Fayol principles of management are presented below.

i.   The Fayol principles of management theories take into account human behavioural characteristics of the company while Taylor principles of management focus on the employee productivity.

ii.   In contrast to Taylor principles of management, which place more emphasis on worker's time and work study, Fayol principles of management place more emphasis on tasks like planning and controlling.

iii.   Furthermore, while Taylor principles place greater emphasis on low-level management in an organization, Fayol principles place more emphasis on the top-level management's perspective on problem solving.

iv.   Taylor principles, on the other hand are mostly used to specialized organizations like manufacturing and engineering. In contrast, Fayol principles can be applied to any organization because they are universally applicable.

REVIEW QUESTIONS

1.   Distinguish between management as an art and management as a science.

2.   List and explain the levels of management.

3.   What are the functions of management? Explain them.

4.   Explain the basic elements of F.W. Taylor contributions to management.

5.   List and explain the principles of management advocated by Taylor.

6.   List and explain the fourteen principles of management advocated by Hendry Fayol.

7.   Give a Comparison of F.W Taylor and Hendry Fayol Theories of Management

CHAPTER 9 FINANCIAL MANAGEMENT

9.1 INTRODUCTION

Financial management is the practice of managing money (funds) effectively and efficiently in order to achieve an organization's goals. It is the specialist role that is most closely related to senior management. The importance of this role is not only apparent in the "Line," but also in the capability of "Staff" as a whole inside a corporation. The management function known as financial management is responsible for organizing, obtaining, and overseeing the firm's financial resources such that the rate of return on investment (ROI) of the organization is maximized.

9.2 NEED FOR FINANCIAL PLANNING

The process of figuring out how a corporation will be able to afford to meet its strategic goals and objectives is known as financial planning. Normally, a business develops a financial plan right away after deciding on its vision and goals.

The following tasks are included in the components of financial planning activity.

- Assessment of business environment and revisiting the vision and objectives of the company.
- Determination of type of resource requirements to achieve the objective of the organization.
- Determination of optimal mix of the resources, viz. men, machine and materials in proportionate to the volume of the business.
- Finding the cost of procurement of the resources.
- Preparation of a budget for resource management through a careful compilation of prices.
- Prediction of risks and problems associated with the budget and formulation of risk mitigation strategies.
- 10   Financial planning is essential to every organization's success.
- 11   It lends the Business Plan rigour by attesting to the reachability of the stated goals from a financial perspective.

9.3 OBJECTIVES OF FINANCIAL MANAGEMENT

The objectives of the financial management are as listed below.

- The basic goal of financial management is to work for profit maximization, which happens if the marginal cost is equal to marginal income.
- It aims to maximize the wealth of the company, which is achieved through maximization of shareholder' wealth, which is a higher-level objective when compared to profit maximization.
- Every effort to minimize capital costs will assure increase in the profit of the operations of the business.
- Financial management should plan for optimal flow of money into the business with utmost consistency.
- It should work towards increasing rate of return of the business, which will be aided through increased earnings, consistent growth in share price and thus pushing the share of the company into blue-chip list, and fulfilling shareholders' expectations.
- It should take sufficient care to optimally use the money that has been sourced.
- To assure safety on investment, the money should be reinvested in safe ventures to earn reasonable return on investment.

9.4 FUNCTIONS OF FINANCIAL MANAGEMENT

The functions of the financial management are as listed below.

i. Predicting capital requirements
ii. Formulation of capital mix
iii. Alternatives of sources of funds
iv. Investment of funds
v. Cash Management
vi. Financial controls

Predicting capital requirements: When determining the company's capital needs, a finance manager must predict them based on the past activities of the business and past cost data to provide enough capital for future activities and projects. Such effort will aid to maximize organization's future earnings.

Formulation of capital mix: After estimating capital need of the company, the company should go in for planning capital structure such that the financial requirements are met in short term, medium term and long term.

Alternatives of sources of funds: The composition of capital structure consists of bond, denture, equity share, retained earnings, etc. Each alternative has an associated cost. Hence, they should be selected in certain proportion such that the cost to the company is minimized.

Investment of funds: After having sourced the fund, the finance manager should allocate the fund to different activities/ projects of the business by taking relative risks into account such that its total return is maximized.

Cash Management: Cash is necessary to fulfill the requirements of paying wages and salaries, different utilities and water bills, creditors, current obligations, providing sufficient stock on hand of cash, procuring raw materials, etc. Hence, management of cash to fulfill all these requirements is an important role of the finance manager of the business.

Financial controls: The financial manager is responsible for managing finances in addition to planning, obtaining, and using funds. The use of funds in different activities of the business should be optimally controlled using ratio analysis, financial forecasting, revising the forecast of fund periodically, cost and profit control, etc.

9.5 EVALUATION OF ALTERNATIVES

In an organization, there will be a situation to select the best alternative course of action from among available alternatives.

The bases for evaluation of alternatives are as given below.

i.   Present worth method of comparing alternatives
ii. Future worth method of comparing alternatives
iii. Annual equivalent method of comparing alternatives
iv. Rate of return method of comparing alternatives

9.5.1   Present Worth Method of Comparing Alternatives

In this method of comparison, the cash flows of each alternative will be reduced to time zero by assuming an interest rate i. Then depending on the type of decision, the best alternative will be selected by computing the present worth amounts of the alternatives.

In cost dominated cash flow diagram, the costs will be assigned with positive sign and the profit, revenue and salvage value will be assigned with negative sign. In revenue dominated cash flow diagram, the profit, revenue and salvage value will be assigned with positive sign. The cost will be assigned with negative sign.

In case the decision is to select the alternative with the minimum cost, then the alternative with the least present worth amount will be selected. On the other hand, if the decision is to select the alternative with the maximum profit, then the alternative with the maximum present worth will be selected.

The assumptions that are made in the present worth method of comparing alternatives are as given below.

- Cash flows are known based on past data and with prediction of future requirements.
- Generally, inflation is not considered in this method.
- The company assumes a realistic interest rate.
- Intangible factors are ignored in this method.
- The organization has sufficient fund to implement the selected

alternative.

The above assumptions are valid for all other bases of comparison of alternatives also.

The revenue dominated cash flow diagram is shown in Fig.9.1.

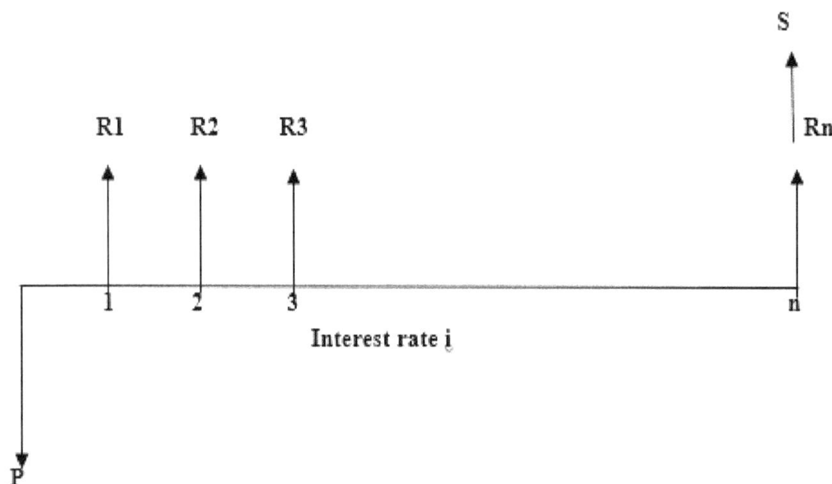

Fig.9.1 Revenue dominated cash flow Diagram

In the Fig.9.1,
n is the life in years of the alternative
P is the initial cost of the alternative
R_i is the revenue accounted at the end of the year i, i = 1, 2,3, ..., n
S is the salvage at the end of the life of the alternative
i is the interest rate

The cost dominated cash flow diagram is shown in Fig.9.2.

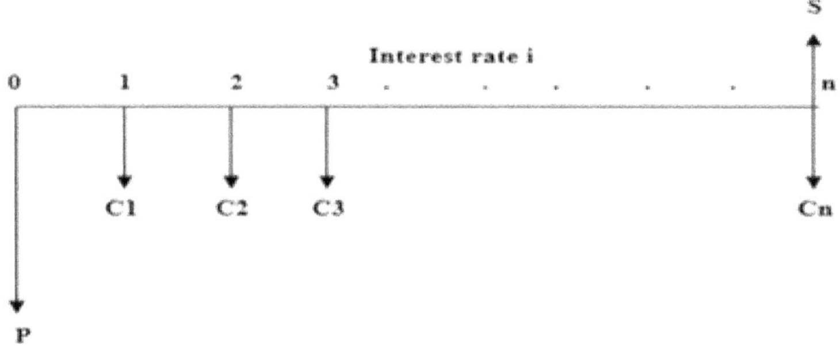

Fig.9.2 Cost dominated cash flow diagram,

In the Fig.9.2,

n is the life in years of the alternative
P is the initial cost of the alternative
Ci is the cost accounted at the end of the year i, i = 1, 2,3, ..., n
S is the salvage at the end of the life of the alternative
i is the interest rate

Based on the Fig.9.1, present worth amount is given by the following formula.

$$PW(i) = -P + \frac{S}{(1+i)^n} + R \times (P\ Given\ R, i, n), if\ R = R1 = R2 = R3 \ldots = Rn$$

$$where, P\ given\ R, i, n = \frac{(1+i)^n - 1}{i \times (1+i)^n}$$

If the revenues at the end of different years are not the same, then, these revenues are to be taken to time 0.

Based on the Fig.9.2, the present worth amount is given by the following formula.

$$PW(i) = P - \frac{S}{(1+i)^n} + C \times (P\ Given\ C, i, n), if\ C = C1 = C2 = C3 \ldots = Cn$$

$$where, P\ given\ C, i, n = \frac{(1+i)^n - 1}{i \times (1+i)^n}$$

If the costs at the end of different years are not the same, then, every transaction is to be taken to time zero.

9.5.2 Future Worth Method

In the future worth method of comparison of alternatives, the future worth values of the alternatives will be computed. Then the alternative with the maximum future worth of net revenue or with the minimum future worth of net cost will be selected as the best alternative for implementation. Future worth analysis is equivalent to present worth analysis; the best alternative one way is also best the other way. There are many situations where we want to know what a future situation will be, if we take some particular course of action now. This is called future worth analysis

Based on the Fig.9.1, future worth amount is given by the following formula.

$$FW(i) = -[P \times (1+i)^n] + S + R \times (F\ Given\ R, i, n), if\ R = R1 = R2 = R3 \ldots = Rn$$

$$where, F\ given\ R, i, n = \frac{(1+i)^n - 1}{i}$$

If the revenues at the end of different years are not the same, then, these revenues are to be taken to the end of the period n and they must be added to S. The value of P also should be taken to the end of the period n with negative sign.

Based on the Fig.9.2, the future worth amount is given by the following formula.

$$FW(i) = [P \times (1+i)^n] - S + C \times (F\ Given\ C, i, n), if\ C = C1 = C2 = C3 \ldots = Cn$$
$$where, F\ given\ C, i, n = \frac{(1+i)^n - 1}{i}$$

If the costs at the end of different years are not the same, then, every transaction is to be taken to the end of the period n.

9.5.3 Annual Worth Method of Comparing Alternatives

In this method, the mutually exclusive alternatives are compared on the basis of equivalent annual worth. The equivalent annual worth represents the annual equivalent value of all the cash inflows and cash outflows of the alternatives at the given rate of interest per interest period. In this method of comparison, the equivalent annual worth of all expenditures and incomes of the alternatives are determined.

Based on the Fig.9.1, the annual equivalent amount(revenue) is given by the following formula.

$$AE(i) = (-Capital\ recovery\ with\ return + R\ ), if\ R = R1 = R2 = R3 \ldots = Rn$$
$$= \{-[(P - S) \times (A\ given\ P, i, n) + S \times i] + R\}, if\ R = R1 = R2 = R3 \ldots = Rn$$
$$where, A\ given\ P, i, n = \frac{i \times (1+i)^n}{(1+i)^n - 1}$$

If the revenues at the end of different years are not the same, then, these revenues are to be discounted to time zero and then P is to be subtracted from them and the resultant value is to be used as P. In such case, R will be absent in the above formula. Then based on the revised P, the annual equivalent amount is obtained.

Based on the Fig.9.2, the annual equivalent amount (cost) is given by the following formula.

$$AE(i) = (Capital\ recovery\ with\ return + C), if\ C = C1 = C2 = C3 \ldots = Cn$$
$$= \{[(P - S) \times (A\ given\ P, i, n) + S \times i] + C\}, if\ C = C1 = C2 = C3 \ldots = Cn$$
$$where, A\ given\ P, i, n = \frac{i \times (1+i)^n}{(1+i)^n - 1}$$

If the costs at the end of different years are not the same, then, these costs are to be discounted to time zero and they must be added to P. The present worth of S is to be subtracted from the resultant value to obtain the net P. Then the net P is used to obtain the annual equivalent cost.

Example 9.1 (Present worth method)

Lakshmi Industry is planning to expand its production operation. It has considered two different brands of equipment to meet the purpose. The initial outlay and net annual revenues with respect to each of the technologies are summarized in Table 9.1. Find the best technology for implementation based on the present worth method of comparison. Assume an interest rate of 10% compounded annually.

Table 9.1 Data of Brands of Equipment

Equipment Brand	Initial outlay (Rs.)	Net Annual Revenue (Rs.	Life (Years)
Brand 1	15,00,000	5,00,000	12
Brand 2	25,00,000	8,00,000	12

Solution

In the comparison of the brands of the equipment, the initial outlay is assumed with negative sign and the revenues are assumed with positive sign.

The cashflow diagram for the brand 1 is shown in Fig.9.3.

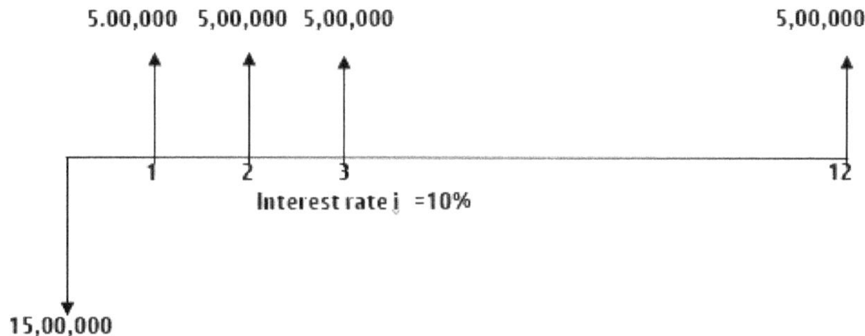

Fig.9.3 Revenue dominated cash flow Diagram for Brand 1 equipment

$$PW1(i) = -P + R \times (P\ Given\ R.10\%, 12)$$

$$where, P\ given\ R, i, n = \frac{(1+i)^{n}-1}{i \times (1+i)^{n}}$$

$$= -1500000 + 500000 \times \left(\frac{(1+0.1)^{12}-1}{0.1 \times (1+0.1)^{12}}\right) = Rs.\ 19,06,846$$

The cash flow diagram for the brand 2 is shown in Fig.9.4.

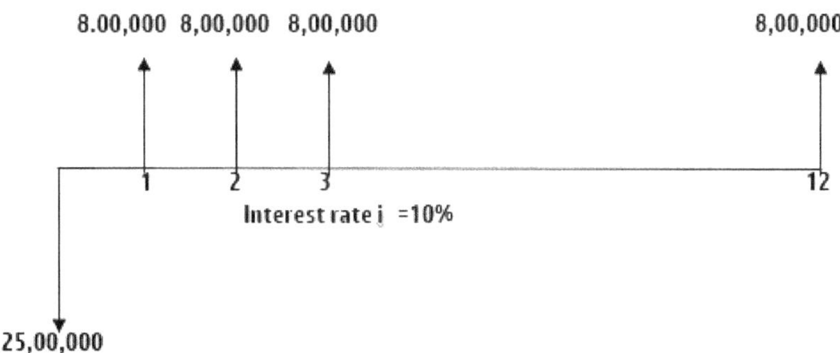

Fig.9.4 Revenue dominated cash flow Diagram for Brand 2 equipment

$$PW2(i) = -P + R \times (P \ Given \ R, 10\%, 12)$$

$$where, F \ given \ R, i, n = \frac{(1+i)^n - 1}{i \times (1+i)^n}$$

$$= -2500000 + 800000 \times \left(\frac{(1+0.1)^{12}-1}{0.1 \times (1+0.1)^{12}}\right) = Rs. 29,50,953$$

The present worth of the Brand 2 equipment is more than that of the Brand 1 equipment. Hence, the Brand 2 equipment is to be selected for implementing the expansion project.

Example 9.2 (Future worth method)

Consider two mutually exclusive alternatives as shown in Table 9.2. By assuming an interest rate of 12%, find the best alternative.

Table 9.2 Data of Alternatives of Example 9.2

		End of year				
	Initial outlay	Net Annual revenue				
		1	2	3	4	5
1	75,00,000	30,00,000	30,00,000	30,00,000	30,00,000	30,00,000
2	60,00,000	25,00,000	25,00,000	25,00,000	25,00,000	25,00,000

Solution

Alternative 1

Initial investment, P = Rs. 75, 00,000
Net annual revenue, A = Rs. 30,00,000
Interest rate, i = 12%, compounded annually
Life of alternative 1 (n) = 5 years
The cash flow diagram of alternative 1 is shown in Fig.9.5.

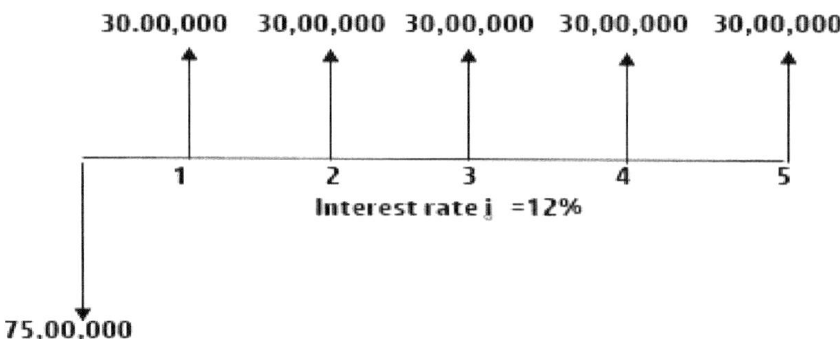

Fig.9.5 Revenue dominated cash flow Diagram of Alternative 1

$$FW(i) = \quad [-P \times (1+i)^n] + R \times (F \; Given \; R, 12\%, 5)]$$

$$where, F \; given \; R, i, n = \frac{(1+i)^n - 1}{i}$$

$$FW1(i = 12\%) = -7500000 \times (1+0.12)^5 + 3000000 \times \left(\frac{(1+0.12)^5 - 1}{0.12}\right)$$

$$= Rs. \, 58,40,979.46$$

The cash flow diagram of alternative 2 is shown in Fig.9.6.

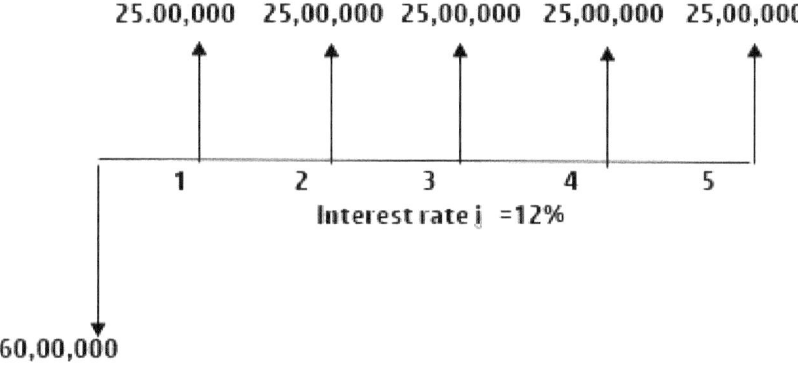

Fig.9.6 Revenue dominated cash flow Diagram of Alternative 2

$$FW(i) = \quad [-P \times (1+i)^n] + R \times (F \; Given \; R, 12\%, 5)]$$

$$where, F \; given \; R, i, n = \frac{(1+i)^n - 1}{i}$$

$$FW2(i = 12\%) = -6000000 \times (1+0.12)^5 + 2500000 \times \left(\frac{(1+0.12)^5 - 1}{0.12}\right)$$

$$= Rs. \, 53,08,068.30$$

The future worth of the Alternative 1 is more than the future worth of the Alternative 2. So, the Alternative 1 is the best alternative for selection.

Example 9.3 (Annual equivalent method/ Annuity method)

A company has to select the best alternative from among the two alternatives, whose details are shown in Table 9.3 using annual equivalent method. Find the best alternative by assuming an interest of 10% compounded annually.

Table 9.3 Data of Alternatives of Example 9.3

Alternative	Initial outlay (Rs.)	Net Annual revenue (Rs.)					Scrap value (Rs.)
		1	2	3	4	5	
1	1,00,00,000	40,00,000	40,00,000	40,00,000	40,00,000	40,00,000	15,00,000
2	90,00,000	35,00,000	35,00,000	35,00,000	35,00,000	35,00,000	12,00,000

Solution

The interest rate is 10% compounded annually.

The cash flow diagram of Alternative 1 is shown in Fig.9.7.

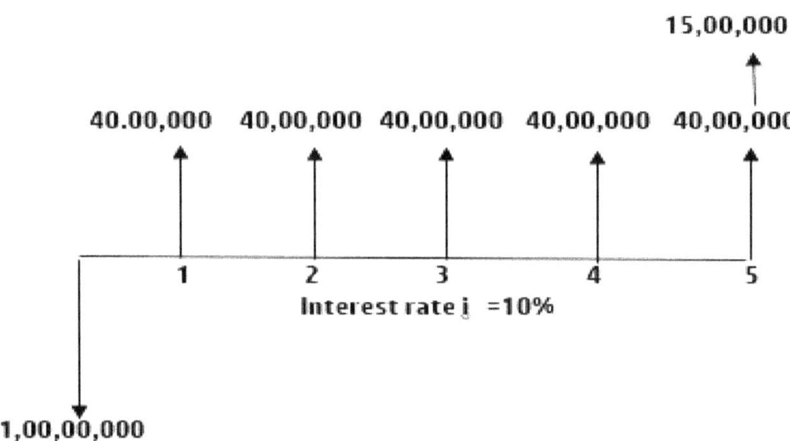

Fig.9.7 Revenue dominated cash flow Diagram of Alternative 2

$$AE(i) = \{-[(P - S) \times (A\ given\ P, i.n) + S \times i] + R\}$$

$$where, A\ given\ P, i.n = \frac{i \times (1+i)^n}{(1+i)^n - 1}$$

$$AE1(i = 10\%) = \left\{-\left[(10000000 - 1500000) \times \frac{0.1 \times (1 + 0.1)^5}{(1 + 0.1)^5 - 1}\right.\right.$$
$$\left.\left. + 1500000 \times 0.1\right] + 4000000\right\}$$

$$= RS.16,07,721$$

The cash flow diagram of Alternative 2 is shown in Fig.9.8.

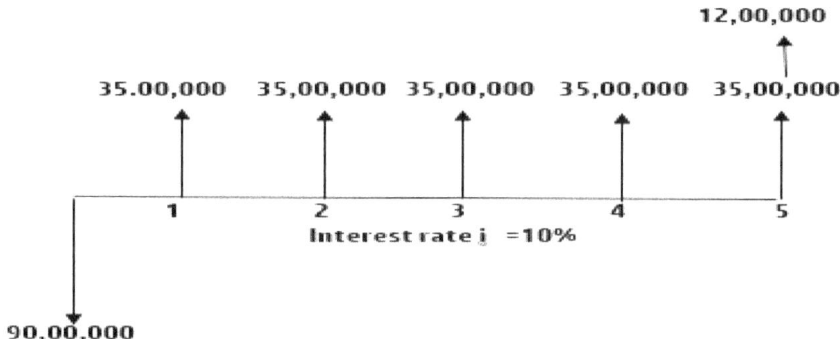

Fig.9.8 Revenue dominated cash flow Diagram of Alternative 2

$$AE(i) = \{-[(P - S) \times (A\ given\ P, i, n) + S \times i] + R\}$$

$$where,\ A\ given\ P, i, n = \frac{i \times (1+i)^n}{(1+i)^n - 1}$$

$$AE2(i = 10\%) = \left\{ -\left[(9000000 - 1200000) \times \frac{0.1 \times (1 + 0.1)^5}{(1 + 0.1)^5 - 1} \right.\right.$$

$$\left.\left. + 1200000 \times 0.1 \right] + 3500000 \right\}$$

$$= RS.\ 13,22,380$$

The annual equivalent revenue of the Alternative 1 is more than the annual equivalent revenue of the Alternative 2. Hence, the Alternative 1 is the best alternative for implementation.

9.5.4   Rate of Return

Return is the financial term for an investment's profit. It can be calculated as a percentage of the total amount invested. A negative return is what you get when there is a loss rather than a profit.

A rate of return is the amount of money that is made on an investment over time stated as a percentage of the initial investment. When the time frame is a year, the rate of return is referred to as the annual return. The rate of return for each choice is calculated in this comparative approach. The optimal alternative is then determined to be the one with the highest rate of return.

The steps of the rate of return method are listed below.

i.   Draw the cashflow diagram of the given alternative.
ii.   Derive the present worth function of the alternative by treating revenues as positive and costs as negative values.
iii.   Guess an initial rate of return.
iv.   Find the value of the present worth function that is devised in the Step ii.
v.   If the present wroth value is positive, go to Step vi; else go to Step vii.
vi.   Increment the rate of return by a meaningful value and go to Step iv.
vii.   Interpolate the rate of return between the earlier rate of return and the current rate of return using the following formula.

$$Rate\ of\ return = Earlier\ Rate\ of\ Retuen + \frac{(Present\ worth\ of\ earlier\ rate\ of\ return - 0)}{Present\ worth\ of\ earlier\ rate\ of\ return - Present\ wroth\ worth\ of\ current\ rate\ of\ return} \times \Delta$$

Where Δ is the difference between the earlier rate of return and current rate of return.

9.6 DEPRECIATION

Any equipment which is purchased today will not work for ever. This may be due to wear and tearof the equipment. Hence it is to be replaced at the proper time for continuance of any business. The replacement of the equipment at the end of its life requires money. It represents the reduction in market value of an asset due to age, wear and tear and obsolescence. The physical deterioration of the asset occurs due to wear and tear with passage of time. Obsolescence occurs due to availability of new technology or new product in the market that is superior to the old one and the new one replaces the old even though the old one is still in working condition. The examples of tangible assets for which the depreciation analysis is carried out are construction equipment, buildings, machinery, vehicles, etc. Depreciation amount for an asset is usually calculated on yearly basis. The recovery of money from the earnings of equipment for its replacement purpose is called depreciation fund since we make an assumption that the value of the equipment decreases with the passage of time. Thus, the word "depreciation" means decrease in value of any physical asset with the passage of time.

Terminologies of Depreciation

The terminologies of depreciation are explained below.

Initial cost is the total cost of purchasing the asset.

Salvage value represents estimated market value of the asset at the end of its useful life.

Book value is the asset's worth as it appears in the company's accounting records at a particular time. Typically, it is determined at the conclusion of every year. The initial cost less the total amount of depreciation up to that year is the book value at the end of the given year.

Useful life shows the anticipated length of time that the asset will be profitable. Even if an asset is still functional after its useful life, it could not be cost-effective. Depreciable life is another name for useful life. The asset loses value during the course of its useful life.

9.6.1   Straight Line Method of Depreciation

In this method of depreciation, a fixed sum is charged as the depreciation throughout the lifetime of an asset such that the accumulated sum at the end of the life of the asset is exactly equal to the purchase value of the asset. It is the simplest method of depreciation. In this method it is assumed that the book value of an asset will decrease by same amount every year over the useful life till its salvage value is reached.In other words, the book value of the asset decreases at a linear rate with the time period. The expression for annual depreciation in a given year 'n ' is presented as follows.

$$D_i = \frac{P - S}{n}$$

Where, n is the life of the equipment in year

      D_i is the depreciation of equipment for the year i, where i varies from 1 to n

      P is the purchase price of the equipment

      S is the salvage value of the equipment at the end of its life.

The book value of the equipment at the end of its life is given by the following formula by assuming B_0 as P.

$$B_i = B_{i-1} - D_i \text{ for i} = 1, 2, 3, \ldots, n$$

Where,

    n is the life of the equipment

    B_i is the book value of the equipment at the end of the year i. i varies from 1 to n

    B_{i-1} is the book value at the end of the year i − 1

    D_i is the depreciation for the year i

Example 9.4

A company has purchased equipment whose first cost is Rs. 1, 25,000 with an estimated life of five years. The estimated salvage value of the equipment at the end of its life time is Rs. 25,000. Determine the depreciation charge and book value at the end of various years using the straight-line method of depreciation.

Solution

Purchase price of the equipment, P = Rs. 1,25,000

Salvage value at the end of the life of the equipment, S = Rs.25, 000

Life of the equipment, n = 5 years

$$D_i = \frac{P - S}{n}$$

Where,

    n is the life of the equipment in year

    D_i is the depreciation of equipment for the year i, where i varies from 1 to n

    P is the purchase price of the equipment

    S is the salvage value of the equipment at the end of its life.

    The book value of the equipment at the end of its life is given by the following formula by assuming B_0 as P.

$$D_i = \frac{P - S}{n} = \frac{125000 - 25000}{5} = Rs.\,20.000, \qquad for\ i = 1, 2, 3, 4, 5$$

The book values of the equipment are computed as in Table 9.4.

Table 9.4 Calculations of Book values

Book value B_0 = Rs.1,25,000		
End of year i	Depreciation D_i (Rs.)	Book value, B_i (Rs.)
1	20,000	1,05,000
2	20,000	85,000
3	20,000	65,000
4	20,000	45,000
5	20,000	25,000

If we are interested in computing Dt and Bt for a specific period (t), the formulas for specific value of t can be used. In this approach, it should be noted that the depreciation is the same for all the periods.

9.6.2 Declining Balance Method of Depreciation

According to this technique of depreciation, the asset's depreciation for the current period will be calculated based on its preceding period. This strategy is practical because it accounts for the fact that depreciation declines over an asset's lifespan as it approaches its earning capacity decreases. In this method, the book value at the start of each year is multiplied by a fixed percentage to calculate the yearly depreciation, which is stated as a fixed percentage of that value. In other words, there is a greater charge for depreciation at the start of the lifecycle and a lesser charge at the conclusion.

The formula for the depreciation using declining balance method of depreciation is as given below.

$B_0 = P$, where P is the purchase price of the equipment which is equated to the book value at the beginning of the year 1.

$$D_i = K \times B_{i-1}, i = 1, 2, 3, \dots, n$$

Where,
n is the life of the equipment
D_i is the depreciation of the equipment for the year i
K is the depreciation rate
B_{i-1} is the book value of the equipment at the end of the year i-1

Example 9.5

A company has purchased equipment whose first cost is Rs. 2, 00,000 with an estimated life of five years.The estimated salvage value of the equipment at the end of its lifetime is Rs. 60,000. Demonstrate the calculations of the declining balance method of depreciation by assuming 0.2 for K.

Solution

Purchase price of the equipment, P = Rs,2,00,000

Salvage value of the equipment at the end of the life of the equipment, S = Rs.60,000
Life of the equipment, n = 5 years
Depreciation rate, K = 0.2

The summary of the calculations of the depreciations and book values of the equipment at the end of various years are shown in Table 9.5. One should note fact that the book value of Rs.65,536 at the end of the year 5 shown in the Table 9.5 is not equal to the salvage of Rs.60,000 as given in the problem statement.

Table 9.5 Summary of Calculations of Depreciation amounts and Book Values

Book value B_0= Rs.2,00,000 and K = 0.2		
End of year i	Depreciation $D_i(Rs.)$ $D_i = B_{i-1} \times K$	Book value. $B_i(Rs.)$ $B_i = B_{i-1} - D_i$
1	$2,00,000 \times 0.2 = 40,000$	1,60,000
2	$1,60,000 \times 0.2 = 32,000$	1,28,000
3	$1,28,000 \times 0.2 = 25,600$	1,02,400
4	$1,02,400 \times 0.2 = 20,480$	81,920
5	$81,920 \times 0.2 = 16,384$	65,536

9.7 Break Even Analysis

The objective of break-even analysis is to find the cut-off production volume for which there will be no profit or no loss.

Let, S be the selling price per unit of a product
  v be the variable cost per unit of the product
  FC be the fixed cost
  Q be the production quantity
  Totals sales (S) = s x Q
  Total variable cost = v x Q
  Total cost (TC) = Total variable cost + Fixed cost = v x Q + FC
  A graph of the break-even chart is shown in Fig.9.9.

The break-even point (BEP) in units is the quantity of sales/ production at which there is no loss or profit.

The formula for the break-even point (BEP) in units is as given below.

$$BEP = \frac{FC}{s - v}$$

where,
        FC is the fixed cost

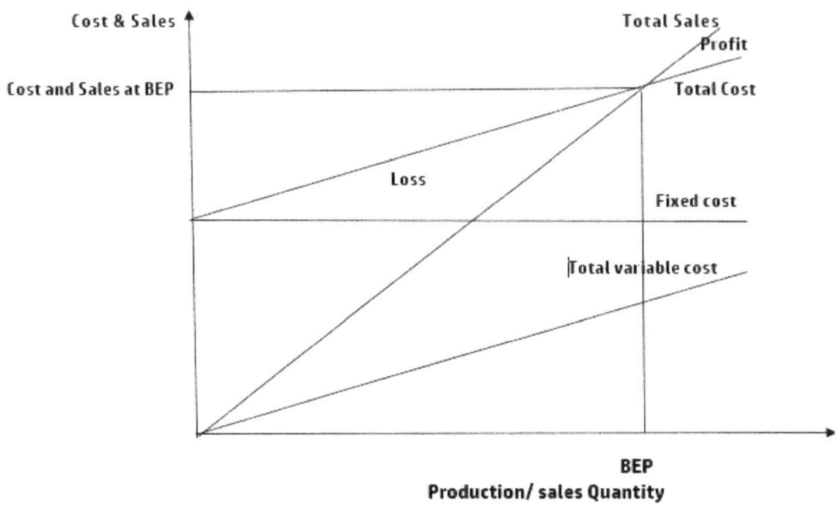

Fig.9.9 Break-even chart

s is selling price per unit

v is the variable cost per unit

BEP is the break-even point in units

Break-even sales= BEP in units x s

The contribution is the difference between the sales and the variable costs.
The margin of safety (M.S.) is the sales over and above the break-even sales
The formulae to compute these values are:

Contribution = Total Sales – Total variable cost

Contribution/unit = Selling price/unit – Variable cost/unit = $s - v$

M.S. = Actual sales – Break-even sales

$$= \frac{profit}{Contribution} \times Sales$$

$$\text{M.S in percentage} = \frac{Margin\ of\ safety\ (MS)}{Sales} \times 100$$

Example 9.6

Beta Associates has the following details:

Fixed cost = Rs. 30, 00,000

Variable cost per unit = Rs. 150

Selling price per unit = Rs. 300

Find

(a) The break-even sales quantity

(b) The break-even sales

(c) If the actual production quantity is 80,000

Find (i) contribution;

(ii) margin of safety

Solution

Fixed cost (FC) = Rs. 30, 00,000

Variable cost per unit (v) = Rs. 150
Selling price per unit (s) = Rs. 300

$$a)\ BEP = \frac{FC}{s-v} = \frac{30,00,000}{300-150} = 20,000\ units$$

$$b)\ Breakeven\ sales = BEP \times s = 20000 \times 300 = Rs.\,60,00,000$$

$$c\ i)\ Contribution = Break\ even\ sales - v \times BEP = 60,00,000 - 150 \times 20,000$$
$$= Rs.\,30,00,000$$

$$c\ ii)\ Margin\ of\ safety = Sales - Break\ ven\ sales = 80,000 \times 300 - 60,00,000$$
$$= 2,40,00,000 - 60,00,000$$
$$= Rs.\,1,80,00,000$$

REVIEW QUESTIONS

1.Define financial management
2. Discuss the need for financial planning.
3. List and explain the objectives of financial management.
4. List and explain the functions of financial management.
5. Explain the following method of evaluation of alternatives.
    a) Present worth method
    b) Future worth method
    c) Annual equivalent method
    d) Rate of return method
6. Alpha Industry is planning to expand its production operation. It has considered two different brands of equipment to meet the purpose. The initial outlay and net annual revenues with respect to each of the technologies are summarized in the following table. Find the best technology for implementation based on the present worth method of comparison. Assume an interest rate of 10% compounded annually.

Data of Brands of Equipment

Equipment Brand	Initial outlay (Rs.)	Net Annual Revenue (Rs.	Life (Years)
Brand 1	30,00,000	9,00,000	10
Brand 2	49,00,000	15,00,000	10

7. Consider two mutually exclusive alternatives as shown in the following table. By assuming an interest rate of 11%, find the best alternative.

Data of Alternatives

	Initial outlay	End of year				
		Net Annual revenue				
		1	2	3	4	5
1	75,00,000	25,00,000	25,00,000	25,00,000	25,00,000	25,00,000
2	60,00,000	20,00,000	20,00,000	20,00,000	20,00,000	20,00,000

8. A company has to select the best alternative from among the two alternatives, whose details are shown in the following table using annual equivalent method. Find the best alternative by assuming an interest of 12% compounded annually.

Alternative	End of year						Scrap value
	Initial outlay (Rs.)	Net Annual revenue (Rs.)					(Rs.)
		1	2	3	4	5	
1	1,20,00,000	45,00,000	45,00,000	45,00,000	45,00,000	4500,000	18,00,000
2	1,05,00,000	36,00,000	36,00,000	36,00,000	36,00,000	36,00,000	14,00,000

10 List and explain the steps of rate of return method of evaluating alternatives.

11 Define depreciation and explain the terminologies used in it.

12 What is straight line method of depreciation? Explain its steps to determine the depreciation of each year and book value of each year.

13 What is declining balance method of depreciation? Explain its steps to determine the depreciation of each year and book value of each year.

14 A company has purchased equipment whose first cost is Rs. 1, 00,000 with an estimated life of five years. The estimated salvage value of the equipment at the end of its life time is Rs. 20,000. Determine the depreciation charge and book value at the end of various years using the straight-line method ofdepreciation.

15 A company has purchased equipment whose first cost is Rs. 2, 20,000 with an estimated life of five years.The estimated salvage value of the equipment at the end of its lifetime is Rs. 70,000. Demonstrate the calculations of the declining balance method of depreciation by assuming 0.25 for K.

16 Give a sketch of break-even chart and explain its elements.

17 Explain the following.
    a.   Define break-even point.
    b.   Contribution
    c.   Margin of safety

18 ABC company has the following details:

Fixed cost = Rs. 20, 00,000

Variable cost per unit = Rs. 120

Selling price per unit = Rs. 300
Find   (a) The break-even sales quantity
         (b) The break-even sales
         (c) If the actual production quantity is 20,000,
             Find   (i) Contribution
                   (ii) Margin of safety

CHAPTER 10 MARKETING MANAGEMENT

10.1 INTRODUCTION

The goal of marketing management is to maximize income for the goods and services a firm sells by controlling its marketing operations, resources, and strategies. Furthermore, the necessity of extending business globally increases the significance of international marketing. The nature of the product, the volume of business, the focus on quality, and the preferences of the customers, among other factors, are the influencing factors that demand different skills in them. So, the marketing managers of the companies should equip themselves with the necessary skills to match the companies with which they are employed. To describe the qualities of the items supplied in the market, marketing executives should be technically skilled; otherwise, buyers may not understand the features of the products, which could result in poor marketing campaigns.

10.2 MARKETING PHILOSOPHY

Every firm may operate under a different set of guiding ideas, which is known as marketing philosophy. Some businesses might wish to operate on a large scale in order to benefit from mass production. Similar to this, some other businesses might be eager to operate on a smaller scale while offering a wider range of goods that appeal to a wider customer base. The following list of marketing principles serves as a guide for the actions of the marketing department's staff and aids in the accomplishment of corporate objectives.

- Production concept
- Product concept
- Selling concept
- Social concept
- Marketing concept

10.2.1   Production Concept

Companies that subscribe to the product concept think that as long as their goods are readily available and affordable, there will be an assured demand for their products and services. A business in this category participates in mass production while maintaining a strong distribution network to meet client demands for the lowest price, highest quality, and shortest lead times.

10.2.2   Product Concept

Companies that adhere to the product concept think that if the items are of the best quality, a large number of customers will naturally be drawn to them. This is based on the fact that the customers are more knowledgeable in terms of cost-effective use of the products due to continued availability after their purchase. These businesses will place a greater emphasis on the production team's ability to make products of the highest quality.

10.2.3 Selling Concept

The marketing axiom that contends buyers won't make special efforts to buy a company's products if they are given the freedom to make their own decisions. As a result, it requires companies to aggressively promote their sales. According to this argument, firms must run extensive, aggressive marketing and sales efforts because if customers were left to make their own decisions, they wouldn't buy enough of a company's items. Businesses use this strategy when they have an excess of a product that needs to be sold to clear their stocks.

10.2.4 Social Concept

When a company is making marketing decisions, social marketing directs them to prioritize the needs of their customers, their operational needs, and their long-term interests. According to this idea, the business should determine the needs, wants, and expectations of its target market before providing the products with the highest satisfaction while still keeping in mind the needs of the general public.

10.2.5 Marketing Concept

The purpose of the marketing concept is to help an organization outperform its competitors by generating, delivering, and providing value to its chosen target market. Target market, customer needs, integrated marketing, and profitability are the four pillars of this idea.

10.3 PRICING

Pricing is a component of marketing, which determines the prices of the products and services that a company offers to its customers such that the total sales revenue is maximized and at the same time the customer satisfaction is maximized. The factors that are considered while fixing the price of a product include manufacturing cost, marketing cost, level of competition in the market, market share, brand and quality of that product.

The objectives of pricing are as detailed below.
i.   The main goal of pricing is to increase the company's profitability.
ii.   Customers should be able to purchase more of the products at the fixed pricing.
iii.   The company should design a strong distribution channel, effective promotion schemes and products with good quality, because these influence the pricing of the product.

10.3.1 Pricing Strategies

The key pricing strategies are skimming pricing and penetration pricing.

Skimming Pricing

Skimming pricing is a method of product pricing in which a company sets its starting price as high as its target market would bear before gradually lowering it. The company reduces the price to appeal to a different, more price-sensitive portion of the population as the demand of the initial clients is met and competition enters the market.

The "skimming" of successive layers of cream, or client segments, as prices decline over time gives the skimming technique its name.

Penetration Pricing

By presenting a new product or service at a cheaper price during its initial release, firms can draw people to it through the marketing tactic known as penetration pricing. A new product or service can enter the market more easily and draw customers away from rivals by offering a lower price.

10.4 CHANNELS OF DISTRIBUTION

A channel is a route made available to sell the product with the aid of intermediaries in order to maximize marketing effectiveness. As listed below, there are various levels of channel distribution.

10.4.1 Direct Channel or Zero Level Channels

Zero Level Channel refers to the situation where the maker sells the product straight to the customer rather than an intermediary.

10.4.2 Indirect Channels

The distribution channel is referred to as an indirect channel when a manufacturer enlists the assistance of one or more middlemen to convey items from the location of production to the location of consumption.

The primary varieties are listed below.

- One level channel
- Two level channels
- Three level channels

Fig. 9.1 depicts a schematic representation of each of the three types of channels.

One Level Channel: This design makes use of no intermediate. Instead of selling the items to retailers or wholesalers in this case, the producer sells them straight to the customer.

Two Level Channels: According to this design, a manufacturer sells the product to a retailer, who then sells it to customers. Here, the retailer buys the product in bulk from the producer and then sells it to customers

Three Level Channels: Wholesaler, a new level before the retailer is added to the Two-Level Channels. The wholesaler procures the product in bulk and distribute them to retailers, who in turn sell the products to their customers.

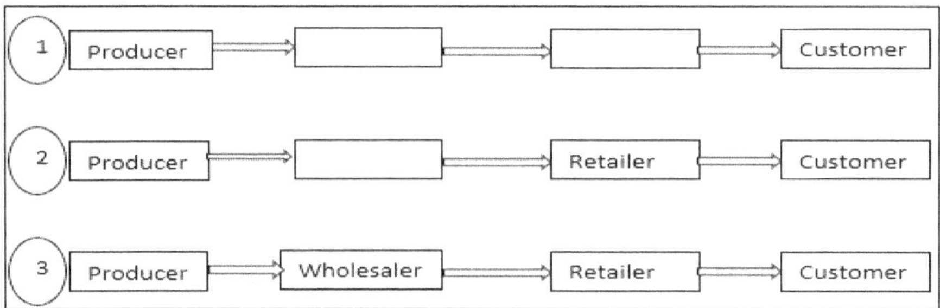

Fig 9.1 Distribution channels

10.5   ADVERTISING

Advertising is a marketing communication that aims to sell or promote a product or service offered by a company to intended customers. Further, it improves the visibility of the company in market circles. The types of advertising include mass media and new digital media. The mass media includes newspapers, magazines, television, radio, outdoor advertising, and the digital media includes direct mail, and blogs, websites, and text messaging, respectively.

10.5.1 Metrics of Advertising

The metrics of importance of advertising are listed below.

i.   *Controlling nature of advertising:* The product launch or conduct of any event of a company can reach customers without any time delay through an appropriate advertising media. The selection and implementing a mix of advertising media can be controlled for a desired advertising effectiveness.

ii.   *Reaching ideal customers:* The advertising message can be designed such that it reaches intended ideal customer segment. This maximizes the effectiveness of the advertisement.

iii.   *Creation of awareness of content for maximal Reach:* The company can focus in creating its content on product details, social responsibilities, best practices followed over years, achievements, etc. through carefully designed eBooks, seminars, magazines, etc. These will create awareness of positive features of a company, its targeted stakeholders, customers and suppliers, educational institutions, which supplies graduates to occupy positions in that company.

iv.   *Drivers of economic growth:* Companies continuously engage themselves in carrying out research and development activities to bring out innovative products and services for maximal profit, which is a compulsion to overcome global competition. Adverting is an efficient tool to take all these messages to intended people, viz. customers, distribution channels of the company as well as to all channels who are involved in similar business to attract them to join hand with the company in future, etc. This would certainly improve the productivity of the company consistently.

v.   *Helping Customer decision:* The customers who buy the product should have complete information on the product, which is possible through effective advertising. The company should establish a brand for the company, which gives confidence to customers while selecting and buying the products of that company.

10.5.2 Types of Advertisement

There are several types of advertising, which are as stated below.

i.   Newspaper
ii.   Magazine
iii.   Television
iv.   Online

Newspaper: Newspaper advertising helps to reach more customers daily in an effective way. The newspaper has classified advertisement and display advertisements. The classified advertisements appear in fixed pages of the newspaper, whereas the display advertisements are scattered throughout the newspaper.

Magazine: The target market of a company can be reached more effectively by placing its advertisement in specialized publications. Such advertisements will help the targeted customers/ readers to read those advertisements according to their own pace and further they keep the magazines for longer period, which will help them to see such adds again, which will have recall effect of the advertisement in the minds of customers.

Television: Since, television has a wide audience, make it as the best medium for advertising if the company serves a sizable market in a border area. In order to convince a buyer to make a purchase from the company, television advertising have the advantages, viz. sight, sound, movement, and colour. Now, a days, recording facilities are present in television, which facilitates customers to review the advertisements that appear in television in future period.

Online: Now a days, many customers access either email or browse some sites of their choice. So, the online advertisement of the product with its features in selecting websites will enhance the reach of the advertisement to a greater extent. The cost of such advertisement is affordable for many companies. So, this medium of advertisement is very much cost effective.

10.6   MARKET RESEARCH

Market research deals with an integrated approach to have an insight into the targeted market of the products of a company. This forms a marketing strategy of the company. Such excise will help the company to win over its competitors in terms of increased market share for its products. The market research provides market needs, level of demand, existing competition, etc. This uses statistical tools to analyze the data more rigorously to test proposed hypotheses relating to the marketing functions of a company. It further helps analyze customer behavior and accordingly the advertisements can be redesigned for maximal reach.

Market information: The pricing of products, and supply and demand situation can be judged more precisely through market information. The market research assists in providing social, technical, and legal factors of markets to intended clients and hence it is an important function of marketing.

Marketing segmentation: Market segmentation forms clusters of customers according to different preferences of customers towards products and services subject to their potential to buy the products of the company.

Market trends: The marketing trend indicates either increase or decrease in the demand of the products and services of a company. There are different models to forecast the demand of a product based on past data. The model that is designed using the past data of a particular method such as regression method will help to compute the size of the demand for a product for which that model is designed. Such estimate help to have seamless integration of the manufacturing facilities with the market demand.

10.7   SWOT ANALYSIS

A SWOT analysis examines a company's strengths, weaknesses, opportunities, and threats. A SWOT analysis should be employed not only during the company's development but also later on in its existence.

10.7.1   Need for SWOT Analysis

The needs for SWOT analysis are as listed below.

i.   SWOT refers to strengths, weaknesses, opportunities and threats. This will help the marketing team to fine tune their activities based on the reality how the given product performs in the market in terms of sales revenue.

ii.   This identifies the internal and external factors which are responsible for the success of the future performance of the company.

iii.   This finds the strengths and weaknesses of the products and the company's internal factors, which are under control.

iv.   The opportunities and threats are the external factors, which are part of the control of the company. But the company should aim to avail the opportunity with a proper caution to mitigate the risk of threats from competitors.

v.   SWOT analysis is carried out as part of the entire corporate planning process, which also includes setting financial and operational goals for the following years and developing strategies to reach them.

The strength dimensions of the SWOT analysis to use resources efficiently are listed below.

i.   One should recognize the fact that every business, even the biggest ones that rule their markets, has a limited amount of capital, staff, and manufacturing capability.

ii.   Assessing the company's strengths helps it to take decision to determine the optimal production quantities of the products according to their priorities such that the revenue and hence the profitability of the company are maximized.

iii.   The identification of the strengths of the company will help it to find the profitable market segments.

The SWOT analysis's Weakness dimensions, if addressed properly will enhance operation performance as listed below.

i.   SWOT analysis identifies weaknesses of a company mainly to analyze and overcome them.

ii.   It identifies the important areas based on the weaknesses to improve operational performance of the company in great magnitude.

The dimensions of the opportunities of the SWOT analysis to identify opportunities are listed below.

i.   The effort to identify new opportunities for the business of a company will bring out new customer group, which is more potential in terms of its buying capacity, extended distribution of products, developing new products to meet unmet needs of customers, expansion of market geographic area, etc.

ii.   Using a SWOT analysis, the management team seeks to foresee longer-term prospects in order to plan ahead and be prepared to enter the market when the time is right.

The dimensions of the threats of the SWOT analysis to cope with risks are listed below.

i.   The threat identified through SWOT analysis means a risk, which is caused by external elements on which the company does not have any control. The primary threats are from the competitors and sometime they may be from other sources too.

ii.   The impact of occurrence of risk on the business may be slow. So, meanwhile, the company should come out with some contingency plan to counter such risks before they become realities.

REVIEW QUESTIONS

1. Define marketing management and explain its importance.
2. What are elements of marketing concept? Explain them.
3. What is pricing? Discuss its objectives.
4. List the key pricing strategies and explain them.
5. What are the levels of distribution channel? Explain them with figures.
6. What is advertising? Explain its need.
7. What are the types of advertising? Explain them in detail.
8. What is market research?
9. List and explain the factors which can be investigated using market research.
10. What is SWOT analysis? Explain its elements.

CHAPTER 11 HUMAN RESOURCE MANAGEMENT

11.1 INTRODUCTION

Human capital is a key resource to put equipment and facilities in an organization to manufacture products for satisfying customer needs. Human resource management (HRM) is a function which administers the human capital to maximize its performance for maximizing organizational productivity. The key functions of HRM are as listed below.

- Hiring employees as per manpower requirement of the company
- Training and development of employees
- Performance appraisal of employees
- Designing reward system for employees
- Designing incentive schemes, etc.

11.2 OBJECTIVES OF HUMAN RESOURCE MANAGEMENT

The objectives of human resource management are listed below.
- i.   Organizational objectives
- ii.   Functional objectives
- iii. Personal objectives

Organizational objectives: HRM is a tool for achieving effectiveness and efficiency in the operations of employees, when they are engaged in their value addition activities in shop floor. This is a function, which embraces all other functional subsystems, operations, marketing and finance, of the organization for their efficient and effective functioning.

Functional objectives: There are numerous tasks that HRM performs for different departments. In the process of supporting all other functions, the cost of execution of the HRM function should be far less than the benefits which would accrue to the organization for the function to be useful to that organization.

Personal goals: The growing global competition needs employees with high talent to take-up the challenges that would emerge in any business. The present competitive industrial scenario would encourage employees to switch jobs from company to company. Hence, the

HRM aims to acquire, develop, utilize and maintain employees for their highest level of performance.

*Social objectives***:** The social issues, viz. legal, ethical and social environmental issues relating to the operation of the business should be attended by HRM. The prim task of HRM is to ensure equal pay for equal work, which will bring harmony among employees.

11.3   ROLES OF HUMAN RESOURCE MANAGEMENT

The roles of human resource management are as listed below.

- Selection of employees
- Training and development
- Placement of employees
- Performance appraisal of employees

11.3.1 Selection of Employees

The selection of employees aims to choose the right men for the right jobs. It is a process for matching organizational needs with people's abilities and credentials. Further the selection chooses the people with required qualifications for the vacant positions in the organization such that maximal match of employees with positions is assured. Such act will assure success of the organization.

Any inconsistency in the selection of employees, particularly when it comes to operational and training costs, can cost a business a lot of money, time, and trouble. The worker can eventually become dissatisfied with their job and leave. He might even disseminate "hot news" and delicious pieces of unfavorable information about the business. Therefore, constant assessment of applicants' suitability for the role is necessary for effective selection.

11.3.2 Training and Development

Training and development focusses on educational activities carried out within an organization with the objective of enhancing an individual's or a group's performance on the job. Most of the activities of training and development concentrate on improving a worker's knowledge and skill sets as well as inspiring more drive to improve work performance.

In this process, the actual required skill sets must be determined first and then the training modules should be designed accordingly to give maximal input for the employees in the training programmes.

11.3.3 Placement of Employees

The placement of employees deals with the practice of assigning a new employee to a position in the organization, which is considered to be potential position for that employee where he/she will have a good chance of success in his career. One can use a *quantitative technique like assignment method, which is a part of Operations Research* to have best matches of the employees with the best jobs such that their contribution to the organization is maximized.

11.3.4 Performance Appraisal

The phrase "performance appraisal" describes the routine evaluation of a worker's productivity and overall value to a business. A performance assessment, sometimes referred to as a yearly review or performance review, assesses the abilities, successes, and growth or lack thereof of an employee. The outcome of the performance appraisal helps the organization to reward employees in terms of recognition and promotions, which will motivate employees to perform better.

11.4 NATURE OF HUMAN RESOURCE MANAGEMENT

The attributes of the nature of human resource management are as given below.

a. HRM aims to bring together employees and organization to achieve the objectives of both parties.
b. HRM is oriented towards end goals of the organization.
c. It strives to support employees to bring out their maximum potential at work place to benefit the organization.
d. It devises systems and procedure to motivate employees to give their best to the organization.
e. It recognizes employees with dignity and treats them well.
f. It recruits and place people in different positions of the organization to achieve its long-term objectives.
g. It assigns right employee to the right job to have maximal productivity.
h. It strives to establish good relationship among the employees of the organization, which will support for synergism in their performance.

11.5 SCOPE OF HUMAN RESOURCE MANAGEMENT

The scope of HRM is as presented below.

- The human resources side focuses on manpower planning, hiring, selecting, placing, transferring, promoting, training and development, layoffs and retrenchments, pay, incentives, etc. for increased productivity of the organization.
- The welfare component is concerned with things like housing, transportation, medical aid, education, health and safety, recreation facilities, and working conditions and amenities like canteens, rest and lunch rooms, etc. to motivate employees to perform better.
- The industrial relations part includes joint consultation, collective bargaining, grievance and disciplinary processes, conflict resolution, and good relations between management and labor unions to have harmony among the employees in the organization.

11.6   GROUP BEHAVIOR

This section presents the aspects of group behavior in an organization, whose dimensions are listed below.

- Interaction among two or more employees at workplace will help to achieve a pre-set goals in an effective manner.
- The effectiveness of the employees will be increased due to group behaviour.
- The members of a group will have more secured feeling because they feel stronger in a group.
- The group behaviour increases the self-worth of its members in an organization.
- The membership of employees in nonwork related groups, viz. study groups, prayer groups, welfare groups, etc. will lead to personal improvement.
- Some member in a group with high level competence may take the role of group facilitator.

11.6.1   Stages of Group Behavior

The stages of the group behavior are as listed below.

i.   Forming
ii.   Storming
iii.   Norming
iv.   Performing

Forming: Forming is the first stage in group formation, which will have more ambiguity in terms of having less confidence to become as members of the group on the part of the employees.

Storming: The second stage of team growth occurs at this point, when the group begins to work things out and win each other's trust. When people express their thoughts, this stage frequently begins. If individuals of the team are given positions of power and authority, conflict may develop.

Norming: Team members are developing fresh approaches to working and playing together at this stage. Leadership shifts from "one" teammate in control to shared leadership as the group becomes more cohesive. Team members come to understand that effective shared leadership depends on mutual trust.

Performing: Performing is the last stage of group behavior, which makes the group functional to deliver its intended tasks. As an example, the quality circle in an organization starts gives solutions to various quality issues of the organization, in specific in manufacturing and distribution activities.

11.6.2 Distinction Among Group and Team

Team and group are distinct from one another. Though a group is not always a team, all groups are teams. The members of a team are highly dedicated to a common objective of the organization, adhere performance standards, and eager to implement strategies for organizational improvements.

A group consists of two or more individuals, who interact with each other in a synergistic manner for supporting organizational activities.

11.7   MASLOW'S HIERARCHY OF NEEDS

Abraham Maslow propounded a theory, which is known as Maslow's hierarchy of needs in philosophy as shown in Fig.11.1.

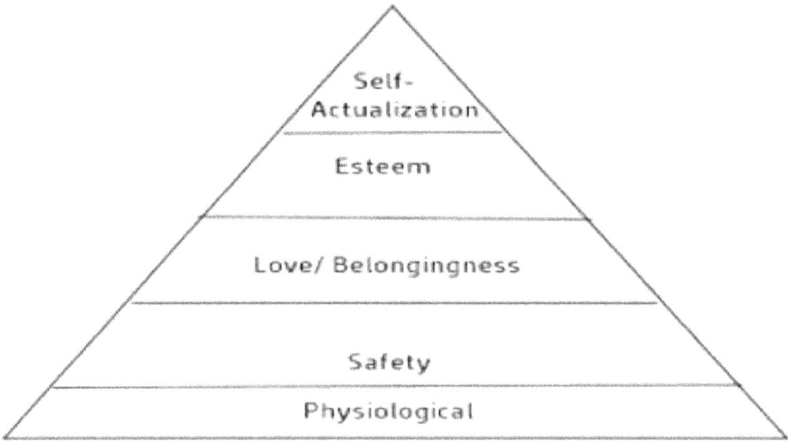

Fig.11.1 Maslow's hierarchy of needs

Maslow expanded his concept to take into account his observations of employees' inborn curiosity. His beliefs are consistent with a wide range of other theories of human developmental psychology. Maslow used the hierarchy of needs from bottom to top of the pyramid as under to characterize the pattern that human motivations often follow.

- Physiological needs
- Safety needs
- Love/ Belongingness
- Esteem
- Self-actualization

Physiological needs: The physical necessities for human survival are called physiological needs. The human body will eventually stop working properly if these conditions are not satisfied. It is believed that physiological demands should come first because they are the most crucial.

Safety needs: Safety needs consist of the following.
    i.   Personal security
    ii. Financial security
    iii. Health and well being
    iv. Safety net against accidents/ illness

i. *Personal security*

Personal security frees employees from any unexpected threat from environment and other sources, which will make them to concentrate on their jobs.

ii. *Financial security*

Financial security means enabling employees to fulfill all financial needs of them and their families, which will make them to excel in their work place.

iii. *Health and well-being*

Health and well-being of employees ranks top priority, because such things will keep the employees with best fitness for work and also their family members in good health.

iv. *Safety net against accidents/illness*

The safety net against accidents/ illness of employees will facilitate their availability to work through avoidance of accidents at workplace.

Love and belongingness: The third level of human needs is interpersonal and encompasses sentiments of belongingness once physiological and safety requirements are met. Maslow asserts that regardless of how big or tiny their social groups are, people need to experience a sense of acceptance and belongingness.

Esteem need: In organizations, it is the expectation of employees that everyone wants to be treated with respect. This includes the requirement for self-respect and self-worth. The basic human desire of the employees in an organization to be liked and valued by others is represented by the need for esteem.

Self-actualization: This level of need is concerned with the attainment of a person's full potential. This level, according to Maslow, is the drive to achieve everything that is possible in order to maximize one's potential. In some employees, it may be a natural occurrence and in others, it may be inculcated through proper orientation.

11.8   JOB ANALYSIS

Job analysis identifies the content of a job in terms of the tasks involved and the qualities or requirements needed to carry out the tasks. Organizations can use information from job analysis to assist them choose the employees who are most qualified for a certain job. The analyst must comprehend the key responsibilities of the job, how they are carried out, and the essential human traits required to carry out the job successfully through job analysis.

The following list contains the goals of the job analysis.

- To identify the best practices for carrying out a task.
- To boost job satisfaction of employees.
- To determine the essential contents for employee training.

- To create job measurement system.
- To find best match of the jobs with employees.

11.9 JOB EVALUATION

A job evaluation aims to assess a job's value or worth in comparison to other positions within an organization. In an effort to create a fair compensation structure, it makes systematic comparisons between tasks to determine their relative worth.

The process for evaluating a job has the following steps.
- Establishment of fair pay differences within the organization for various positions according to the contents of the jobs that are performed by the employees.
- Doing away with salary disparities among the employees.
- Ensure that all eligible employees are paid the same amount for similar work.
- Establish a bench system to create career planning for the employees of the organization.

11.10 MANAGEMENT BY OBJECTIVES

Management by objectives (MBO), often referred to as management by result, is the process of creating organizational goals so that management and staff members are on board with the goals and are aware of what needs to be done in the company to attain them.
- Management by Objectives (MBO) is a human resource strategy, which facilitates managers and employees to collaborate for establishing, documenting, and tracking goals over a period of time.
- MBO sets precise organizational goals which are to be communicated to team members and provides ways and means of achieving those goals.
- MBO encourages participative goal setting, determining an effective plan of action and decision making.
- MBO establishes a system of measuring and comparing the performance of employees against benchmark standards. If employees are part of setting benchmark standards, there is a greater possibility of achieving the bench mark standards by them at workplace,
- MBO facilitates employees to observe their own accomplishments, which motivates them to excel in their performance in future.
- MBO helps managers to assign specific goals to their subordinates and achieve them with their commitments.

11.10.1 Features, Merits and Demerits of MBO

The features, merits and demerits of MBO are presented in this section.

The features of MBO are listed below.

- Motivating employees through involving employees in goal setting and providing an opportunity for employee empowerment.
- Frequent interactions among the employees and reviews between managers and their subordinates improves the working relationship

among them and solve many operational issues.

- MBO helps to establish charity of goals of the organization for employees.
- Since MBO empower employees in goal setting, it increases the commitment of them towards their jobs.
- The superior in an organization work towards linking subordinates' goals with the organizational objectives.

The merits of MBO are listed below.

- o MBO has several clear benefits. It offers a way to set goals and make plans to achieve them.
- o Planning enables proactive behavior and a methodical approach to achieving goals.
- o Measurable goals make it simple to evaluate and modify them.
- o If goals are effectively created, managed, and attained, organizations can also increase productivity, conserve resources, and boost morale.

The demerits of MBO are as given below.

- o The MBO process increases comparisons between individuals at the workplace.
- o In order to outperform their coworkers, employees frequently rely on ugly politics and other useless practices.
- o Employees solely carry out the instructions of their superiors.
- o MBO leads to lack of innovation and creativity, and introduces monotonous work nature.

REVIEW QUESTIONS

1. Define human resource management and explain its objectives.
2. Discuss the roles of HRM.
3. Discuss the roles of human resource management.
4. Discuss the dimensions of HRM.
5. Give the scope of HRM.
6. What is group behavior? Explain its aspects.
7. List and explain the stages of group behavior.
8. Explain the differentiation between groups and teams.
9. Give an account of group dynamics.
10. Give the levels of Maslow hierarchy needs and explain them.
11. What is job analysis? Explain its objectives.
12. What is job evaluation? Explain the procedure for this analysis.
13. What is management by objectives?
14. Discuss the features of MBO.
15. List the merits and demerits of MBO.

REFERENCE

1. https://keydifferences.com/difference-between-fayol-and-taylor-theories-of-management.html#:~:text=Fayol%20is%20oriented%20towards%20managerial, is%20termed%20as%20Engineer's%20approach.
2. https://www.businessmanagementideas.com/production-management/procedure-for-method-study-6-steps-production-management/9719
3. https://www.economicsdiscussion.net/engineering-economics/charts-used-in-motion-study-5-types/21703
4. https://www.intechopen.com/chapters/54334
5. https://www.leansixsigmadefinition.com/glossary/simo-chart/
6. https://www.mindtools.com/pages/article/newTMM_Taylor.htm#:~:text=Taylor's %20philosophy%20focused%20on%20the,simplifying%20jobs%2C%20productiv ity%20would%20increase.
7. https://www.onlineclothingstudy.com/2011/03/how-to-do-time-study-for-garment.html
8. https://www.quora.com/What-is-a-string-diagram-and-what-is-the-purpose-of-a-string-diagram
9. https://www.simplilearn.com/principles-of-management-by-henri-fayol-article
10. https://www.simplilearn.com/principles-of-management-by-henri-fayol-article#:~:text=Henri%20Fayol%20was%20known%20as,%2C%20Commanding% 2C%20Coordinating%20and%20Controlling.
11. Panneerselvam, R. and Sivasankaran, P., Process Planning and Cost Estimation, PHI Learning Private Limited, Delhi, 2016.
12. Panneerselvam, R. and Sivasankaran., Quality Management, PHI Learning Private Limited, Delhi, 2014.
13. Panneerselvam, R., Engineering Economics (2nd Edition), PHI Learning Private Limited, Delhi, 2013.
14. Panneerselvam, R., Operations Research (2nd Edition), PHI Learning Private Limited, Delhi, 2006.
15. Panneerselvam, R., Production and Operations Management (3rd Edition), PHI Learning Private Limited, Delhi, 2022.
16. Panneerselvam, R., Senthilkumar, P and Sivasankaran, P., Computer Integrated

Manufacturing: Automation in Manufacturing, Cengage India Pvt. Ltd., Delhi, 2020.

17. Sivasankaran, P. and Shahabudeen, P., 2013, Modeling Hybrid Single Model Assembly Line Balancing Problem, Udyog Pragati Vol.37, No.1, pp.26-36.

18. Sivasankaran, P. and Shahabudeen, P., 2014, Literature Review of Assembly Line Balancing Problems, International Journal of Advanced Manufacturing Technology, 73, 1665-1694.

19. Sivasankaran, P. and Shahabudeen, P., 2014, Study and Analysis of GA-Based Heuristic Applied to Assembly Line Balancing Problem, Journal of Advanced Manufacturing Systems, 13(2), 113-131.

20. Sivasankaran, P. et al, 20010, Heuristic to Minimize Makespan in Uniform Parallel Machines Scheduling Problem, Udyog Pragati, Vol.33, No.3, pp.1-15.

21. Sivasankaran, P. et al., 2010, Efficient Heuristic to Minimize Makespan in Single Machine Scheduling with Unrelated Parallel Machines, Journal of Intelligent Information Management, Vol.2, pp.188-198.

22. Sivasankaran, P. et al., 2010, Design and Comparison of Simulated Annealing Algorithm and GRASP To Minimize Makespan in Single Machine Scheduling *with Unrelated Parallel Machines*, Journal of Intelligent Information Management, Vol.2, 406-416

23. Sivasankaran, P. et al., 2011, Literature Review of Single Machine Scheduling Problem with Unrelated Parallel Machines, Udyog Pragati, Vol.35, No.3, pp.1-15.

24. Sivasankaran, P. et al., 2011, Mathematical Modelling of Single Machine Scheduling Problem with Uniform Parallel Machines to Minimize Total Tardiness, Industrial Engineering Journal, Vol.II, No.2, pp.39-44, 2011.

25. Sivasankaran. P, 2021, Quality Concepts in Industrial Systems Using QFD – Survey, International Journal of Industrial Engineering, Vol:8, Issue 1, pp.7-13.

26. Sivasankaran. P, Shahabudeen P., 2013, Genetic Algorithm for Concurrent Balancing of Mixed Model Assembly Lines with Original Task Times of Models, Intelligent Information Management 5(3): 84 -92.

www.ingramcontent.com/pod-product-compliance
Lightning Source LLC
LaVergne TN
LVHW060557200726
843509LV00003B/145